America's Dilemma:

Alone *or*
Allied?

America's Dilemma:
Alone *or* Allied?

by

Norman Angell

HARPER & BROTHERS *Publishers*

New York *and* London

327.73
A58

CONTENTS

CONTENTS

vi

CONTENTS

America's Dilemma:

Alone *or* Allied?

Chapter I

WHY THIS BOOK

The lessons which Europeans did not learn and which concern Americans. Why the European witness should not be ruled out. A personal note on this present witness.

This book suggests that the fate of Europe points certain very plain lessons which America ought to take to heart, first, in her own obvious interest, and secondly in the interest of that relatively free and humane civilization of which she is a part, and in the collapse of which she would be involved. The book is written in the conviction that if she does not learn those lessons, this kind of civilization must go under as it has already gone under in so much of the world, and be replaced by one less free, less humane; a kind which may last a very long time, as other slave societies, like that which built the pyramids, lasted much longer than any of the freer types which the world has known.

I

AMERICA'S DILEMMA:

The author tries to show that it is futile to blame upon one wicked man, or one wicked government, or one wicked people, the fate which has befallen Europe. If two men can sit in a railroad carriage in the Brenner Pass—as they are sitting at the moment that these lines are being written—deciding in secret the fate of the world, deciding, without consultation of any kind with any of them, what shall be done with the lives of hundreds of millions of human beings (the previous decisions of these two men, or of one of them, having already vitally affected the life of every family in America, as these pages show) it is because those millions have not yet learned how to manage their society; have not yet learned self-government. The power of a Hitler is the measure of the political incompetence of the multitudes with whose lives he plays so recklessly.

This book tries to show that the European peoples—and very particularly the British—have fallen into that paralysis or impotence by reason mainly of the misunderstanding, or disregard of certain principles which lie at the root of all organized society; that this disregard has been due

2

largely to certain prejudices which are also strong, in slightly different form, among the people of this country (as of all countries) and are likely deeply to sway the vital decisions which America must now make in relation to the march of Nazi power.

An outstanding feature of the story of the Western democracies, as this last ten years shows, is that governments were often prevented from doing what they knew to be the right thing at the right time, because they would have met with such intense popular opposition, an opposition which often disappeared as events proved the need of the measures in question. But by the time that events had demonstrated the need of a given measure, it was, in instance after instance, too late for the measure to be effective: events had now moved beyond its scope. No feature of Europe's collapse is more common, and more striking, than this time lag between what the situation really called for at a given moment and what the public were ready to sanction.

But the importance of public understanding of foreign policy goes beyond the matter of timeliness—of doing the right thing before it is too late.

3

As against any step some considerations can be urged. Political action is never a choice between what is entirely good and advantageous and entirely bad and disadvantageous, but depends upon a balance of considerations. And a relatively good policy may fail if it is applied halfheartedly; if the public is deeply divided as to its wisdom. The success of a country's foreign policy may depend, less upon its intrinsic merit at every point than upon the degree of popular support which it can win, so that the government applying the policy can do so with speed, decision, persistence. A defective policy so applied might win out where an abstractly better one applied late, indecisively, with hesitations and vacillations, would fail.

The recent history of Europe gives ample illustration of this truth. Part of the "lesson of France" is, obviously, that the country was divided as to the policy which led it into the war; had been divided for years, hesitant as to whether Berlin or Moscow were the greater danger; confused as to the issues on the Spanish matter; some doubting even the value of the British alliance and wondering whether France was not being used as a cat's-paw for the protection of interests which were not at

4

bottom hers. On these points there was no real unanimity.

The country, it is true, wanted to defeat Hitler, would have been glad of victory over him. But it wanted other things too: peace, preservation of the country's solvency; some protection against a Communism which Germany's defeat might cause to expand. So that when war finally came internal divisions weighed very heavily; there were intrigues; confusion as to just what ought to be paid for victory, what sacrifices were justified. To say that we want something, as Frenchmen wanted continued political independence, does not really mean much. Every desired end has almost always to be paid for by the sacrifice of some other desired end, as a man sacrifices desired leisure for a still more desired successful career or business. The things we get for nothing are usually worth what we pay for them.

Americans today desire the defeat of Hitler. But they—rightly—want to know the price; and many are profoundly convinced that the price which they are being asked to pay as a contribution to that defeat is neither justified nor necessary; many feel they are being asked on quite inadequate

5

grounds to abandon treasured traditions, to neglect the lessons of their own history, and of quite recent experience.

The overwhelming majority of Americans have today great admiration for Britain's struggle and wish her well, and are prepared to give such help as they can without becoming involved.

Very many are determined, however, to have no war for themselves, no repetition of the futility of 1917-1918 when they gave of their best for a victory which was to make peace and democracy secure for all time, only to find a few years after victory that those things were more insecure than ever. They ask questions which this book elaborates. If the last victory was all undone in a couple of decades, how long would a new one endure? They feel that they were made the victims of an astute British propaganda; that the declared aims of the war were not the real ones, which probably had closer connection with Britain's imperial and the Morgans' financial interests than the public were allowed to know.

It might, Americans feel, be even worse next time. Complete defeat of Germany would, some fear, mean revolution and chaos in that country, in which case Russia, who has already absorbed more than half of Poland, a large part of Roumania, some of Finland, the whole of Lithuania, Esthonia and Latvia, and immensely increased her strength and improved her strategic position, would dominate the situation, and, given the unrest and instability of the government in France, push through to the Atlantic coast. Bolshevist supremacy would thus extend across half the world from the Bering Strait (within a gunshot of American territory) to the Straits of Dover. Most Americans feel that if Hitler is bad as master of the Old World, Stalin would be worse.

America's first duty, they insist, is therefore the preservation of her own democracy and peace, her own soil. This she can accomplish if she concentrates upon it to the exclusion of foreign adventures. By such concentration, they argue, she can make the country impregnable, invasion certain to be defeated, foreign domination, humanly speaking, impossible

Such a case seems to many Americans unanswerable on any ground of legitimate American interest.

AMERICA'S DILEMMA:

This book proposes to answer it.

For a year or two now one of the main activities of this writer[1] has been to try to persuade his countrymen that the issues in this war do not divide on national lines but on lines which intersect frontiers; and that we shall lose unless we recognize the implications of that truth; if we continue to assume that all Germans are on one side in the struggle and all Frenchmen on the other; that in this world-wide revolution a man's sympathies are necessarily determined by his legal nationality; that the Jew or the Social Democrat escaping from Dachau or Buchenwald to Britain must then be regarded (as British policy did for a time and very disastrously regard him) as an enemy because he is "German"; that the Germany of Einstein or Thomas Mann is just the same as that of Streicher or of Himmler; that Britain under Churchill, Morrison, Bevin, Greenwood, Dalton must be regarded as the same Britain as the Britain of Chamberlain, Simon, Hoare; that the Britain which has so readily made Canada an independent nation is exactly the same Britain which fought the thirteen col-

[1] See particularly the author's *We and the Refugee*.

8

onies.[2] Yet just that assumption is the habit of much current speech and writing.

But the point compels a personal note.

The author of this book was born in England, received some of his education at a French lycée, some at a Swiss university; has lived twenty years of his life on the continent of Europe (mainly France); and some ten years in the United States.

The fact that the author of the book is a European will at once, in the minds of some Americans, condemn him as a prejudiced witness who should not be heard at all in the discussion of American policy. That condemnation itself, however, begs and prejudges at the outset the very question which we ought to examine open-mindedly: are there certain basic interests common to all free societies that can best be defended by common action, co-operatively? To say, in relation to that question, that no European should listen to an American, and no American to a European; that exchange of ideas between them

[2] "Britain, since the day George Washington made her a refugee from America, has never ceased to wish us evil and has at all times worked venomously against us." From a leading article in the New York *Enquirer*.

on that point is "insidious," or corrupting, or subversive, is to advance the strange proposition that we should not attempt to profit by the experience of others, should not, in estimating experience, hear "the witnesses who were there." Consider a moment. Strange, incredible disasters have happened in Europe; Americans desire to avoid those disasters and to that end want to know how and why they happened to others. Is it seriously suggested, therefore, that they should not listen to those who happened to be in the thick of those events for fear that somehow "propaganda" should slip past? The counsel would seem to place a very low estimate on the perspicacity of Americans, and a very high estimate on their gullibility.

While yet in his teens this present writer left the Swiss university at which he was studying and emigrated to America, where for five years he earned his living by manual labor: as a farm hand, a cowboy, later as a prospector, in this country and in Mexico. After that came some time as a reporter on Western and Southern newspapers. While still a hired hand on a farm he took out his "first papers," with the intention of becoming an American citizen, an intention later frustrated by the fact that family reasons compelled his return to Europe. There his life has been divided between journalism in France and Britain, much travel on the Continent (including Germany), membership of the British House of Commons, much political writing, most of it extremely critical of the policy of the British government—as the record shows.

The reader must judge whether that background, which includes five of the formative years of youth spent in manual labor in America (and consequently in an environment where so many of the roots of America are to be found), furnishes sufficient justification for presenting to Americans the considerations which follow.

A final word as to the method of this book.

In the next chapter the author is not stating his own views; he is acting as reporter, trying to state, fully and fairly, as convincingly as he possibly can, the case which he essays to answer.

He has adopted this method, not with any idea of engaging in an amusing intellectual game, but because in the difficult job of discovering the truth that method, in certain circumstances, affords the best chance of seeing it.

Chapter II

THE CASE FOR AMERICAN ISOLATIONISM

Why should the next victory to make the world safe for democracy be any more successful than the last? The defeat of German Nazism might put Russian Bolshevism in control from the Bering Sea to the Straits of Dover. Would American help to Britain go the way of British help to France? Professor Beard's view. Colonel Lindbergh's. Does Britain's fleet protect America? The appeal to history. America is impregnable—if she stays at home.

When middle-aged Americans are told that their country must now take its part in "the fight for civilization," to "save democracy," they are likely to recall the fact that twenty-five years ago they were asked to do that selfsame thing; that they agreed; entered the war, and, at the cost of turning the whole nation's life upside down, and diverting the course of its development, achieved, or helped to achieve, victory.

But the victory then achieved at such enormous cost in treasure, in the disorganization of natural life, with its subsequent miseries of depression and unemployment, did not make the world safe for democracy. On the contrary, Allied victory was followed by a world-wide repudiation of democracy; a veritable epidemic of dictatorships; a counter-revolution against freedom and democratic ideals such as modern times had never before known. Victory did not bring peace to the world—obviously. It did not give this country—or any other—political security, for we are now told that America is more insecure than she has ever been in her history.

But if all that is the result of the last victory, what grounds have we for supposing that the next victory is going to give results any more satisfying? If the previous victory for democracy has to be fought all over again at the end of two decades, how long is the next victory going to last? If that victory was all undone in twenty years, how long is the next going to endure?

Wilson's tragic struggle with the old-world diplomacy suggests that though American power may ensure victory, it is impotent to ensure its proper use. And looking at Europe today, many

Americans feel that it would be far more difficult now than it was then to ensure the proper use of victory, for the political situation is even more complicated than in 1918. German defeat would probably involve revolution—indeed revolution may be one of the arms which the democracies will employ for their liberation from Nazi domination. But Russia will be nearer in every sense to that revolution than the Western democracies can be; in a much better position to determine its direction. One of the grave possibilities of the situation is that German defeat and revolution might make Russia master of the European continent, acting through subversive parties which exist in every European state. If Russian Communism could take charge of the revolution in Germany it could almost certainly extend it to France, where the reactionary, quasi-Fascist government with its Nazi-like policy will have prepared the soil for violent proletarian uprising. This would mean dominant Bolshevism over nearly half the universe.

No one, of course, can know with any certainty whether this will happen. But equally can no one say that it is impossible; and in any case it is not the kind of situation in which America can usefully intervene.

And could there be such a thing as victory? What would victory mean?

The Allies went to war to save Poland. Does anyone suppose that Germany, having been defeated and her half of Poland having been restored, the Allies will then proceed to make war upon Russia in order to restore the other half? Or to restore Finland? Or the Baltic republics, set up by the Allies in 1918 as a *cordon sanitaire* against Russia and which Russia has now absorbed? And would it be a work of "democracy" to restore Poland to her dictators and agrarian grandees? Or to restore France to the men of Vichy?

All the conditions which made it impossible for America to use victory, even when she achieved it, for the purpose of making the world safe for democracy, have become intensified since the outbreak of war in 1939. The vast uncertainties of military alliances have been illustrated in this present war as perhaps never before in history. The Grand Alliance which won the last war did not outlast victory a decade. First

Japan fell away, then Italy, both ultimately join-ing the erstwhile enemy. And then one by one all the lesser states fell away from the anti-Ger-man combination, some through sheer destruction by Germany, as in the case of Poland, others by fear of what would happen to them at the hands of Germany if they remained part of the anti-German combination. There remained France and Britain. This partnership at least looked secure. England gave of her best; she poured vast materials of war, nearly all such trained soldiers as she possessed, into France. But the event proved that France could not in fact be saved; could not in a sense be helped. For there were elements in France which did not believe that the interests of the two countries were identical; they believed, perhaps quite sincerely, that Brit-ain was using France as a cat's-paw for purely British purposes; there were those who believed that as between playing second fiddle to Britain and second fiddle to Germany, there was not much to choose; in either case France's inde-pendence was qualified, compromised. German propaganda played astutely on all these doubts with a success that very few in England thought possible. The end of it was, not merely that France dropped out of the war, making, in violation of her undertaking, a separate peace, but did so in conditions which made it possible for Germany to use the vast military resources of France—her airplane and munitions factories, her coal and iron—against England. The very guns and shells, the vast equipment which Britain had sent so lavishly to France for the purpose of fighting Germany, were turned by Germany against Britain; Britain's own arms became instruments for her destruction. The French navy itself would have been so used, had not Churchill taken the tragic, the appalling decision to seize it by force at the cost of French lives.

If that could happen as between France and Britain, who had co-operated formally as associates or allies for forty years; who had fought the last war from the very first day together; who had made peace at the same table—if an alliance of such obvious mutual advantage and urgency could thus disastrously break down, what assurance have we that an Anglo-American alliance would not be subject to equal strain? That the same thing in only slightly different form might not happen and that we might not see American ammunition and planes and ships used against America for the destruction of American ships and lives, as the British have seen British ammunition and planes used against British ports and cities and British lives? Are we so sure that Britain does not contain anti-American elements just as France contained anti-British? That just as there were quasi Fascists, Lavals, and Flandins, in high places in France ready to make a deal with Germany at Britain's expense, there may not be Fascists, anti-aliens, anti-Semites, in high places in Britain prepared, when things go badly, to let down America as France let down Britain?

To suggest this, is not to indict the whole British nation, any more than to recognize the existence of the men of Vichy in France is to indict the whole of France. France may one day rise again to throw these men out; but that must be the work of Frenchmen. Meanwhile the conditions of war fought by international alliance have brought these men to the top, have placed what remains of France within their power, acting as the tools of Germany. We have to face the possibility of this strange phenomenon being repeated in the case of Britain.

Which brings one to the tradition with which the interventionists would seem to want to part company.

The people who built up this country came here to get away from Europe—from its hereditary nationalist animosities, its age-long feuds, retaliations and counter-retaliations. Most of those who came here in the country's early years had suffered bitterly from just those things; intended to leave them behind and establish here a society of a different order in which racial and nationalist hates should have no part. It was this feeling—the feeling that Americans ought to be free of that evil heritage—which formed a great part of the "ideology" of the eighteenth-century revolution, and later caused the country to promulgate a doctrine severing the entire Western Hemisphere from further European rivalries. To keep aloof from those ancient quarrels, to refuse to take sides in them, is counsel which comes to the republic from its founders, advice with which every American schoolboy is familiar. And which seems particularly apposite these days.

AMERICA'S DILEMMA:

One recalls how, in that farewell address which is part of the education of young America, the country was warned so sharply against taking sides in foreign quarrels.

> Excessive partiality for one foreign nation and excessive dislike for another, cause those whom they actuate to see danger only on one side, and serve to veil and even second the arts of influence on the other. Real patriots, who may resist the intrigues of the favourite, are liable to become suspected and odious; while its tools and dupes usurp the applause and confidence of the people to surrender their interests.

And the advice so often quoted:

> Against the insidious wiles of foreign influence (I conjure you to believe me, fellow citizens), the jealousy of a free people ought to be constantly awake; since history and experience prove, that foreign influence is one of the most baneful foes of republican government. But that jealousy, to be useful, must be impartial, else it becomes the instrument of the very influence to be avoided, instead of a defence against it.

Modern point has been given to these counsels by eminent contemporary historians, like Professor Beard; by men like Colonel Lindbergh and a host of statesmen and writers.

Colonel Lindbergh's words are particularly striking. He does not hesitate to declare that for long America has been grossly misinformed about the situation in Europe. "Anyone," he says, "who takes the trouble to read through back issues of our newspapers cannot fail to realize what a false impression we had of the belligerent nations." We were told that Germany was ripe for revolution, that her rearmament was a bluff, that she lacked officers, that she flew her airplanes from one field to another so they would be counted again and again by foreign observers. We were informed that Russia had the most powerful air fleet in the world, that the French army was superior to any in Europe, that the British navy was more than a match for the German air force, that Germany lacked enough food, fuel and raw material to wage war, that the Maginot Line was impregnable, that Italy would never enter a war against England. "Statements of this sort have issued forth in an endless stream from Europe, and anyone who questioned their accuracy was called a Nazi agent."

"These examples," he insists, "show how greatly we have been misled about the military condition in Europe. If one goes still further back," Colonel Lindbergh insists, "he will find that we have also been misled about political conditions. It has seemed obvious to me for many years that the situation in Europe would have to change, either by agreement or by war. I hoped that we had reached a degree of civilization where change might come by agreement. Living in Europe made me fear that it would come only through war."[1]

And there was, in his view, no doubt as to what it was all about.

It is not, he insists, the support of "democracy," or the so-called democratic nations would have given more assistance to the struggling republic of postwar Germany; nor a crusade for Christianity, or the Christian nations of the West would have carried their battle flags to the confiscated churches of Russia; or the preservation of the small and helpless, or sanctions would have been followed by troops in Abyssinia, and England

---

[1] Note from the address delivered in Chicago, August 4, 1940.

would not have refused to co-operate with the United States in Manchuria. He adds:

> The issue is one of the oldest and best known among men. It concerns the division of territory and wealth between nations. It has caused conflict in Europe since European history began.
>
> There is a proverb in China which says that "when the rich become too rich and the poor too poor, something happens." This applies to nations as well as men.
>
> When I saw the wealth of the British Empire, I felt that the rich had become too rich. When I saw the poverty of Central Europe, I felt that the poor had become too poor.

Professor Charles Beard[2] takes a line strikingly parallel to that of Colonel Lindbergh, insisting indeed that the misinformation of the public of the United States stretches back throughout the years. He, too, stresses the economic motivation of policy, but insists that it is a misinformed motivation. He challenges the view that the foreign trade of the United States is either intrinsically important, or that it can be promoted by mixing in foreign quarrels—particularly in the Far East.

"For years Western merchants and their intellectual retainers, including consular agents, filled

[2] Harper's Magazine, September, 1939.

23

the air with a great noise about how much money could be made in China as soon as four hundred million customers got round to buying automobiles, bathtubs, typewriters, radios, refrigerators and sewing machines." Probably, adds Professor Beard, a few of these myth makers were honest. But many among them must, he thinks, have realized that this swarm of customers had neither the money nor the goods with which to pay for Western gadgets. "However that may be, and despite tons of diplomatic notes, despite gunboats, marines, soldiers, Open Doors and all the rest, the trade of the United States with China has been and remains relatively insignificant; in an absolute sense it is of no vital importance to the United States."

Professor Beard, like Colonel Lindbergh, insists that intervention for political ends is as futile as for economic. First, the country has not, and perhaps cannot have the necessary information. Does anyone, he asks, in this country really know what is going on in Europe, behind the headlines, underneath the diplomatic documents? Is it true, as French publicists contend, that the Pope, having blessed the triumph of Franco in Spain, is striving for a union of Fascist and other powers, for the secret purpose of liquidating Soviet Russia? Had Russia just grounds for distrusting the governments of Chamberlain and Daladier? If Hitler and Mussolini are liquidated by pressure or by war, will the outcome be a Victorian democracy, a communistic revolution, or a general disintegration? Are not the powers immediately and directly entangled in all this strife in a better position to adjust their disputes than an American President and his assistants in the State Department?

And so he concludes:

> It is folly for the people of the United States to embark on a vast and risky program of world pacification. We can enjoy the luxury of hating certain nations. We can indulge in the satisfaction that comes from contemplating a war to destroy them. We can rush into a combination that might temporarily check them. But it seems to me, it would be wiser to suggest that those countries of Europe which are immediately menaced by Germany and Italy put aside their jealousies, quarrels, and enmities, and join in a combination of their own to effect control over the aggressors. If countries whose very existence seems at stake will not unite for self-protection,

how can the United States hope to effect a union among them? After temporary pacification what? After war what? After peace what? To these questions the Roosevelt foreign policy makes no answer. And they are fundamental questions.

Mr. Upton Close also thinks there has been systematic distortion of history in the press of late particularly in respect of the role of the British fleet as "America's first line of defense." He thinks this simply turns history upside down. He reminds us that

> The British navy tacitly assisted the rebellion against the Union in 1860-64. Its decks were cleared to crack Lincoln's blockade of the Confederacy when caution took the counsels in Parliament. So far from protecting the Monroe Doctrine at the moment when we were least capable of enforcing it, the British fleet gave Napoleon III the green light to transport a large French army and his puppet Maximilian across the Atlantic to Mexico. Britain took advantage of the situation to turn the self-governing community of British Honduras into an Empire colony. After our War between the States the British fleet did not protect us from anything —there was nothing to protect us from save the British fleet, which President Grover Cleve-

land and Congress kept out of Venezuela (1887, and again 1895-99) by threat of war. In 1902, so far from protecting the Monroe Doctrine from other nations, a British squadron sailed along with German and Italian squadrons to the blockade of Venezuela. Theodore Roosevelt did not rely on the British navy when he insisted that the Venezuelan dispute go to the Hague Tribunal (1902). He relied on the fleet that flies the Stars and Stripes—which quite alone has historically been the reliable keeper-out of this hemisphere of European empire-builders.

It is true, he says, that "a couple of retired admirals—to the disgust of other admirals active and retired" have "so far forgotten their history and training as to join in voicing the absurdity that this nation and hemisphere have been 'protected' by the British fleet." He adds:

They were brought up in quite an opposite tradition. The inner policy of the American navy since it has had a policy and a respectable existence, has been and continues to-day to match the British navy not to trust it. Our navy could never be sure what the British navy would do, or when another Lord John Russell would control it (as in 1863). And so our navy heads insisted against bitter British opposition on complete equality with British sea power in the naval ratio conferences of 1922, 1930 and 1932—and jealously combatted the British objections to our superiority in capital ships.

If ever we have depended upon the British fleet to protect our interests such a policy is not on record—nor is present state policy. Haven't we had enough in newspaper columns and from platforms?

Mr. Close asks whether America could be any more sure of Britain than Britain was of France? "Politicians and Admirals are being arrested in England too. England, also, has gone totalitarian, with no bothersome written constitution to be replaced. Victory would not bring back the England some of us supposed we would be fighting for—the England that we thought was like us."

America has had her sympathies before.

The Reign of Terror aroused American horror then as the trampling of the Jews does today, the Napoleonic conquests inspired passionate outcries against militarism and tyranny as Hitler's blitz-conquests do today. There were extreme pro- and anti-French, and anti-English groups. "But the advantages of America were saved for us because American leaders remembered whence they had come and whither they were bound, and resisted the wolf-in-sheep's-clothing ideological temptations. Jefferson hated kings, but he saw that America could not remove kings from Europe. Let alone and kept out of America, kings would cancel one another out, or otherwise remove themselves. Where it was within the realm of practical statesmanship, Jefferson relieved European potentates of New World territory, and consequently of temptation to build empires or bring war over here."

Mr. Close simply does not believe that the United States can be persuaded that its interests can be best served or dangers averted by joining its destiny to that of the British Empire.

> Psychologically as well as historically the effort is wrong. You cannot put stamina into the American people by telling them that their destiny is tied up with a foreign empire over whose policies they have no control, about whose moves they have always been skeptical with more than a little reason—a power that promises to need saving every twenty years, and that muddles into dreadful scrapes ad interim.

What, he asks, is really involved in the conquest

of Britain by Germany. His answer is sufficiently interesting to be worth quotation:

> Germany has already won its main objective, which was to put England finally and definitely out of Europe—to end any English alliance on the continent that enabled England to say who might and who might not master the politics, resources and business of the European continent. This is a turnover in history like the passing from the Grecian to the Roman world in the ancient Mediterranean. Old nations and empires are climaxing long trends of self-destruction as new forces are arising. The formula is old: it happened to the Persian empire—once so vigorous under Cyrus, to Grecian cities, to Rome, to Spain. All that is needed is for members of the ruling class to become more interested in their private fortunes than in their countries, and for the ruled not to care. In a great structure, like Rome or Britain, self-destruction takes time.
>
> Can anyone condemn an American viewpoint of our interests? Can our English friends, whose government always has and always will put its selfish interests—as it sees them, even when it sees them wrongly—before every consideration of sentiment (as witness Manchuria and Czechoslovakia) condemn us? Can the American believe that if internal weakness and rottenness

and the blindness of his statesmen had brought destruction upon the United States and its democracy, from, say across the Pacific, the British navy would be steaming to our rescue—and that it would repeat the rescue in each generation?

He ends by asking what will be the attitude of American youth who will have to do the fighting. He thinks that Jane Sargent, speaking up in the New York *World-Telegram*, speaks for them truly:

> The young are willing to fight. But with weapons, not words. They are unafraid, but they demand a fighting chance. They demand of their government equality in arms. They do not want to be sold as the French people were. And, also, they will die willingly upon the altar of democracy—for their United States. But never for the British Empire.

The conclusion in Professor Beard's words is that "not until some formidable European power comes into the western Atlantic, breathing the fire of aggression and conquest, need the United States become alarmed about the ups and downs of European conflicts, intrigues, aggressions and wars."

To share that view does not, Mr. Close thinks, exclude the giving of material aid to Britain:

> To build, without more folderol, the world's most modern military machine—one that the mere thought of approximating will break Hitler's heart—that is the basic wisdom of self-preservation. Thus far Hitler hasn't got to America, but in view of the chance, however remote, that he might get around to it, we shouldn't be tempting him by leaving this hemisphere wide open. To weaken him by providing Britain with material while she is still fighting him (but watching lest the stuff fall into his hands, as did much material sent to France) is the sort of simple cunning required of any nation which hopes to survive.

All the foregoing assumes—it is the basic assumption of the isolationist case—that this country, standing alone, can make itself impregnable. And, indeed, there is very weighty technical support for the view that direct invasion of the United States is beyond the bounds of military practicability.

As recently as May 15, 1940, the Senate Committee on Naval Affairs published a report based on a re-survey of American national defense problems under then existing world conditions. Its conclusions, which represent composite opinions derived from responsible naval authorities, military men, members of the air force and informed students of national defense, included the following points, among others:

1. In the military sense the United States is an insular nation and can be defended upon the seas.

2. An insular nation cannot be defeated if it is able to maintain command of the sea and air approaches to its shores and its vital trade routes.

3. The United States at the present time is not vulnerable to direct attack by any means whatsoever save those with which a thoroughly modern navy and air force can deal adequately.

4. Air power, due to its limited radius of action, has not yet changed the fact that . . . we are an insular nation and that we are not vulnerable to direct attack if we prevent the establishment of air bases in this hemisphere.

5. The instrumentalities of war required to make reasonably sure that we shall not be threatened or attacked are: A navy sufficiently strong to meet and defeat any potential enemy before he reaches our shores; an army and air force of sufficient strength to give our navy freedom of action; and the necessary secure bases from

which our fleet and air forces can operate effectively.

The Committee also pointed out that we are not capable of fighting against major opponents in both oceans at once; that we may have to sacrifice our interests in the Far East in case of a British defeat in Europe.

A publication of the Foreign Policy Association points out that before invasion could be undertaken, it would be necessary to destroy the American battle fleet, probably on this side of the Atlantic, and to secure sea and air bases in the Western Hemisphere. To transport an army of even 300,000 men and their equipment across the Atlantic, on the basis of our World War experience would require about 580 average-sized merchant ships, totaling 3,600,000 tons. Such an expedition could hardly be prepared in secret; it would be vulnerable to damage by submarines, mines or aerial bombing, and would be confronted by naval and air forces fighting in well-known home territory and backed by an unrivaled industrial plant. The commentator adds: "There is substantial evidence to show that such an enterprise is beset with obstacles so formidable

34

as to render it unlikely under any conditions we can foresee today."

After all, in this matter of the possibilities of invasion, there are facts of history, both European and American, upon which to base conclusions.

During the last World War complete command of the sea was in Britain's hands; the Belgian coast lay thirty miles away; the landing of Allied armies would have turned the German flank. In the four years of the war, it was never even attempted. Other landings in the face of shore defenses proved, as we know, disastrous failures.

Taking a longer view, we have seen immensely powerful continental states with armies established within twenty miles of the English coast, completely fail at invasion: the failures go back nearly a thousand years. Napoleon's failure has now been followed by Hitler's.

On this side of the world the United States has twice defeated invading armies which have managed to secure a foothold, the armies of an empire completely commanding the sea, an empire so powerful that Napoleon himself, dominating a

Europe more extensive even than that which Hitler now dominates, could not defeat it. What Napoleon could not do, defeat the British Empire, American armies did in the days of America's weakness, when her population was less than a third of that of her enemy. In the second of these wars of invasion the commander of the invading force was decorated for having got his army out of America at all: previous invading commanders had not managed it.

In neither the Revolutionary War, nor in the War of 1812, had this country the particular superiority which evidence seems to show is the determining factor in modern war: the factor of mechanization. The instruments of modern war are mechanical, based on efficient industrial organization. America is the most mechanically efficient nation that the world has ever known.

"Where else," asks a leader writer,[3] "is a Ford who could imagine making 1000 airplanes a day, give him the standard design and let him be? It is only American industry that is able to say to its Government: 'Tell us what you need, give us priority of materials and transportation, and it

[3] In the *Evening Post* of July 20, 1940.

36

shall be produced, anything in any quantity.' We can," continues the writer, "make 1000 tanks a day; a warship a week if need be. Give the machine-tool industry the specifications and let it alone, and we can make guns with the fingers of women.

"Our productive power," he goes on, "is equal to that of all Europe, and may be increased, so far as we know, without limit. Is it something that does not exist? That, too, shall be produced. We have private industries whose research laboratories are unequaled in Europe."

Mechanized warfare suggests that as a people, more than any other, Americans have the feeling of machines in their hands, as you might take for granted, seeing that Americans have and use three-quarters of all the automobiles in the world. They are probably, too, the most air-minded race.

Nor is that all.

First, we are the most nearly self-contained nation of modern times, an empire, possessing of our own in plenty practically every essential thing, including now rubber, which we can make from petroleum. We have no food problem, no umbilical cords to defend. Fewer than one third the number of people now engaged in agriculture could produce an abundance of food.

Statistically measured, we have more than two fifths of all the ponderable, natural, dynamic wealth of the world. We produce more than two fifths of all the steel in a steel age. We have nearly 60 percent of the world's oil. That is to speak of materials. What else?

We have the finest and most highly engined machine craft. Our genius for the technics of mass production is incomparable. Other nations learned mass production from us.

In the view of very many there is just one thing which might possibly render this country vulnerable: transfer of material—planes, ships, artillery, ammunition—to Britain in such quantity as to deplete unduly American stocks. That—also in the view of many—is the final argument for defensive isolationism rather than quixotic interventionism.

Chapter III

THE TREACHERY OF MASKED WORDS

What is "intervention"? And what is "defense"? What does America defend? Hitler is already enforcing drastic changes in America's way of life. How America is following the British road of the last ten years.

Very great confusion in the discussion of foreign policy arises from the fact that we continue to use certain words which have altogether lost the meaning they may once have had as though they still possessed that meaning—clear, precise, exact. "War," "peace," "intervention," "independence," "Empire," "overseas possessions," are only a few of many such. We talk of "keeping out of war," of maintaining "isolation" as against "intervention," remaining at "peace" as opposed to "getting into the war."

Well, China, some of whose closely packed cities have become reeking shambles, nightmares of devastation and horror, is, if you please, at "peace." Japan insists upon it. There is no war. The events there are only part of a prolonged "incident." The killing of hundreds of thousands of Chinese civilians, and reduction of millions to homelessness, is merely "the establishment of a New Order in Eastern Asia." Russia marches her armies into Finland in "response to the appeal of her downtrodden workers" and in order to help the Finnish people "throw off the yoke of the capitalist oppressor." Not only Russians, but many Communists the world over, accepted this as a simple statement of fact; the words, that is, have a meaning in their minds, just as words used the other day by a Communist, when he declared that "the only country in the world where the press is really free, and men can live without fear is Russia," must (to him at least) have had meaning. In destroying the Czechoslovak republic and installing German government in the capital, Germany is not conquering the country, which would once have been the case, she is "taking Moravia and Bohemia under her protection." She also takes a dozen other nations like Norway and Holland, under her protection, in order to "liberate them from the intolerable oppression of Great Britain which they have suffered for so long"; just as the concentration camps and the pogroms are the means by which "the long-suffering German people have at last been freed from the oppression of world Jewry." And Dr. Goebbels solemnly proclaims to his applauding people that "the day of Europe's freedom will have dawned when Britain is defeated." And it is not merely Germans, it would seem, who find some meaning in such phrases. Quite a number of eminent, high-minded and sincere Americans seem to accept the Goebbels picture of a certain "person"—John Bull—being too rich, and "owning" too much, "possessing" too large an "estate" which includes such "property" as Canada. Canadians will be interested to learn that they are the "property" of some "person" who is in a position to sell them. (It was proposed only a few years ago by an American Senator that Great Britain should dispose of this part of her "property" in exchange for a full discharge of her debt to the United States.)

One could go on endlessly with examples of the way in which in political discussion we slip

unconsciously into the use of terms so grossly misleading as utterly to distort our thought, distor-
tions which often end by landing us into a world
of pure fantasy, peopled by nonexistent persons
(John Bull, Uncle Sam) dealing in nonexistent
things (the "ownership" of such "property" as
Canada) title to the "possession" of which can be
transferred from one owner to another.

Something of the same strange confusion
marks terms now so common in discussion of foreign policy in America. America, say the "isolationists" must not "intervene" because the country should preserve its complete freedom from
European entanglements, remain independent of
European disputes, isolated; and to this end
avoid acts of war, giving, however, all aid to
Britain short of war; and should use all her power
to defend herself, not others.

Now, if the words are to be accepted in their
ordinary sense, the policy—upon which all political parties in America, except the Communist
party (so far) have agreed—of giving aid to one
side and refusing it to the other is intervention.
Moreover it will be interpreted as "an act of
war" by Germany at the precise moment which

she, not American isolationists or interventionists, decides. We know from repeated experience that if Germany decides that it is to her advantage to attack a country, she does not wait for it to commit "acts of war"; that she will make anything or nothing an "act of war"—as illustrated in her relations with, say, Denmark and Holland. Nothing could have been more abjectly subservient than Holland's "neutrality." It had no tiniest effect in even deferring the blow of actual invasion. In this case, also, there was no "war," although thousands perished in a bombardment of Rotterdam.

When, therefore, the charge is made that Britain wants to "get us into the war," it is well to remember that it is Germany, not Britain, who will decide when America is "in" the war. Germany would have decided that this country was "in" long since had she deemed it to her advantage so to decide. As to Great Britain "trying to get this country into the war," there is one simple act of Britain that would almost certainly and almost immediately get this country into the war. That act is to be defeated; to submit to Germany, surrender, thus bringing about the establishment of a "Vichy" government, handing over to Germany the British fleet and factories and war resources of Britain. Then indeed would British policy be likely to involve this country in war.

But this country should not, we are told, entangle itself with Britain for then Americans would no longer be complete masters of their policy; it would be decided partly by British partners.

Is America then "free" to decide her way of life *now?* Is she independent of outside influence *now?* The point is worth a little examination.

No American family with a son of military age can have any doubt now that it has already been profoundly affected by what has been happening on the other side of the world. Before any invasion has taken place or even immediately threatened; before any declaration of war, before any dark forces have "got us into the war," strange new features have entered into the "American way of life" as the direct result of decisions made in Berlin, Rome and Tokyo. The decisions made by those foreign statesmen have already grievously encroached upon the freedom of every American citizen.

Heretofore, perhaps, the hard-driven private citizen—the salesman, or farmer, or dentist, or storekeeper, or artisan—struggling to keep out of debt, to keep (or find) a job, to bring up his family decently, has usually been pretty skeptical concerning the value of "the freedom that our fathers gave us" and still more of the talk of "the collapse of civilization" and the dangers of this or that political philosophy. At every election he has been accustomed to hear each party declare that the other is bent upon the ruin of the country; that if that other gains power, it will be the end of prosperity, security, freedom; the country will face dire perils and miseries. And afterwards, when the party of disaster (each party is the party of disaster in the eyes of the other) wins, things go on much as before; much as they would, the citizen suspects (once the ardors of the election have cooled), if the other party had come to power. "The more it changes, the more it is the same thing." Plain John Smith has been for the most part fundamentally skeptical about

45

the importance of political changes as affecting his daily life.

But with the introduction of peacetime conscription, with expenditures for defense so astronomical that they are hardly calculable, with nearly every industry becoming directly or indirectly a defense industry and so, for military reasons, brought under government control, the thing takes on another color. Junior's career is going to be profoundly affected; his life is not his own to the degree that it would have been without this measure; the parents share the son with the government; the state and the state's power over him seem to grow and grow. The state, not his parents, not his inclinations, will determine what he shall do at certain critical junctures; the power that the state now has over him will affect vitally his choice of profession; his marriage perhaps, and so the life of the woman whom he marries or might have married. And he shall learn the art of killing scientifically, killing men, it may be, as good as himself; and shall have no choice about it. And, that, after all, has its spiritual importance.

And on the economic side, will ruefully reflect millions and millions of American John Smiths—or Hans Schmidts—this immense new taxation will make it still more difficult to keep the little business going. And with Schmidt the German name now will have an importance it never had before. Neither Schmidt (nor his neighbors) had ever before thought of himself as anything but American. But now, with the "anti-alien" rampage, with employment agencies demanding "Anglo-Saxon" background, it makes a difference.

Truly indeed have things altered. Heretofore, one had looked upon all this sort of thing—the. compulsory military service in peacetime, the power of the drill sergeant, the presence of government in every sphere of life, the vast public debts, the animosities of national groups within the nation—as European not American, as belonging to the Old World from which it has been the whole purpose of America—of those who left the Old World to make a new one—to get away. And here it all is again in our midst.

But no political party with any faintest hope of winning a majority of American votes dare proclaim that these measures are quite unneces-

47

sary; that the country is in no danger from the growing power of the Axis. True, here and there a man of great independence and boldness, like Colonel Lindbergh, not aspiring to office, will have the temerity to declare of the Axis nations that "if we do not interfere with their affairs none of them will desire to invade us." Yet, even he contradicts this statement when he urges that it is vital for the country to arm ever more heavily; a course which would have no object if there were no danger from others.[1]

Rearmament is regarded all but universally as the only alternative to submission. Our "average citizen" knows too well that the nation is being nazified (it has been pointed out over-plentifully, he thinks, of late) without ever having been conquered by the Nazis. But he knows also that no

[1] And even Colonel Lindbergh recognizes that he does not express predominant feeling in this matter, for in the same speech he adds: "I have a different outlook toward Europe than most people in America. In consequence I am advised to speak guardedly on the subject of war. I am told that one must not stand too strongly against the trend of the times, and that, to be effective, what one says must meet with general approval.

"There is much to be said for this argument, yet, right or wrong, it is contrary to the values that I hold highest in life. I prefer to say what I believe or not speak at all. I would far rather have your respect for the sincerity of what I say than attempt to win your applause by confining my discussion to popular concepts. Therefore, I speak to you today as I would speak to close friends rather than as one is supposed to address a large audience."

single public man dare suggest outright the only possible alternative, which is submission; and that the American public would not dream of accepting such alternative if it were suggested.

And Smith—or Schmidt—admits that the country has no choice. Both parties, all parties, men and women of all opinions agree, that the measures of defense ought to be taken. Some would have relied more on the voluntary system, some would have delayed conscription; some would have persisted longer on the line of appeasement; some would have kept more material at home and given less to enable Britain to keep the enemy on the other side of the Atlantic, but the least informed knows that any party which proposed submission to foreign rule would simply be snowed under. It would be destroyed if it adopted a platform proclaiming: "We will not resist any enemy who cares to invade us and take over the government of this country, as the governments of so many countries heretofore independent have been taken over by one or other of the dictators; we will submit without resistance, as Denmark submitted to one dictator, Latvia, Lithuania and Esthonia to another, Albania to a

third." Indeed, no party proclaiming such doctrine could ever be formed. These military measures which we have adopted are truly hateful,
truly burdensome, are truly transforming the
"American way of life" (Smith is getting a little
tired of the term). But the alternative, he sees
quite clearly, would be still worse, something
which he could not possibly accept. The government has no choice. It is not a free agent.

And that perhaps is the most astonishing re-
flection of all—that the country is not a free
agent; that the people have imposed upon themselves these sometimes hateful things because a
neurotic Austrian house painter has in a sense
commanded them; has adopted certain policies
which make these things necessary. Certain treasured freedoms which America has lost, have been
lost because of things happening at the extrem-
ities of the earth, in China, Japan, Europe. Is
this the "isolationism" of which we hear?

It is no longer possible to argue that if you
leave other nations alone they will leave you
alone; that if you will mind your own business
they will mind theirs.

Did Denmark, or Holland, or Norway go

sticking their noses into Germany's business? Was their foreign policy provocative or quarrelsome? Did they threaten Germany? We know that these ancient nations (the democracy of the Scandinavian states which was sung even in the Icelandic sagas goes back centuries beyond the English Parliament of Simon de Montfort) adopted toward Germany a submissiveness which of recent years had at times developed into the most abject servility. The long course of submissiveness, appeasement, neutrality, made not one iota of difference when it became to the advantage of Germany to conquer their territory, to apply to their people all the characteristics of Nazi rule—the Gestapo, the concentration camp, the press control, the radio control, the censorship of religion, the deportation of "non-Aryans"—not a feature has been missing. There was no declaration of war. German troops were already in occupation of the soil of most of these countries before the "negotiations" began. If the claim in the case of Norway was that there had been unneutral acts, no such claim was even advanced in the case of Denmark. And of late all these pretenses about "unneutral acts" have been dropped. The New

Order is on the march—the New Order being the domination of Germany—and those who would "oppose the course of history" (incidentally, a new kind of national offense) will be overcome and crushed. Anything which might assist "history" will be done without any by-your-leave.

And this brings us to the sovereign word of all in this discussion: defense. We think commonly perhaps as with so many of the other words in this discussion that its meaning is self-evident, clear.

Yet *what* do we defend?

In the preceding chapter most of the authorities quoted seem to insist that America's power should be used only for the defense of the nation's "soil," or the "soil" of this hemisphere. The implication seems to be (and this is particularly so in the writings of Professor Beard), that this country should therefore no longer attempt to defend its commercial or other interests overseas (as in China) or the security of its citizens there; or the security of its citizens on the seas, or those "neutral rights," that "freedom of the seas" for the defense of which this country has actually in the past gone to war on three occasions. We know indeed that in this war, the United States, by withdrawing its ships from the belligerent zone, has surrendered the effort to maintain positions which have been maintained throughout American history with such persistence and such passion, positions which have heretofore been regarded as part of the "great American tradition." The abandonment of those positions is of course a very considerable retreat before advancing violence.

It is obviously important in any discussion of defense to know what is being defended.

Presumably, when we speak of the defense of American soil, we include in it American institutions, "the American way of life"—control of government by the mass of the people, having, for the purposes of that control, access to the facts; the right to discuss them freely and publicly, the "right to know," the right of the people in the light of that knowledge to be masters of their own destiny to decide what shall be done with them, their lives and the lives of their children; their right to be free.

New things of that order may be surrendered

—we have seen it happen repeatedly in Europe —while the "soil" is inviolate so far as foreign soldiery is concerned. We have seen cases in which a people have, from one day to another, surrendered a deeply treasured way of life, the political institutions of a long history, before ever a foreign soldier set foot in their land; and we have seen that change made, not dirctly by the conqueror at all, but by groups within the nation making the change. The soil, in these cases, was "defended," it saw no foreign soldiers; there was peace, no bloodshed, war was avoided; but the nation's most characteristic institutions were completely, unconditionally, surrendered; and destroyed.

The case of unoccupied France is only the latest example of a whole series of cases in which institutions and way of life have, as it were, been traded for inviolability of soil, where invasion has been avoided by a bargain with the enemy along the lines: "Keep your soldiers off the actual soil of this territory and we will agree to make the way of life that goes on within it precisely what you would desire" (and thus the abolition of the Third Republic, the erasure of the nation's watchword, "Liberty, Equality, Fraternity," the Nazi treatment of the Jews).

It will be said: that kind of thing happens only when a nation's bastions are already down, its defenses already destroyed, when it has lost the power to defend itself.

That is quite untrue. It happens when a nation, even a great and powerful nation, has lost a clear sense of things it should defend; of what *is* defense. It happens when a nation begins to think that it can defend its way of life merely by defending its own soil, its physical territory.

The kind of bargain just described as having been made by France has not these last few years been peculiar to beaten nations; nor even to the Czechoslovakia of the period between Munich and the occupation of Prague; nor to Denmark and other small countries. It was in fact the kind of bargain which Britain had been making for years with Germany, Italy and Japan. There were certain things which for generations every Englishman had regarded as indispensable to Britain's way of life, with the maintenance upon the soil of the island of a much larger population than its food resources could nourish. To

55

this end communications with English-speaking democracies at the antipodes sending Britain wool, and wheat and meat, had to be kept open. To defend that "life line" two wars had in the past been fought in order to prevent the establishment on the Spanish peninsula of any power that might cut the line. Yet when Germany (with Italy) made it clear that she proposed to establish herself on the peninsula, that is to say to set up in conjunction with Italy a puppet government in Spain which she could dominate, she made it clear that Britain must abandon her ancient claims in respect to the Mediterranean route, or face war. But in fact the British government said, as it had said repeatedly when faced with similar situations in the recent past—in Manchuria, in China proper, in Abyssinia, in the Rhineland—"Our first task must be to avoid becoming involved in war, to keep war from our shores, our soil, our cities. These are the things we have to defend. If we intervene in this struggle, between the Spanish government and the rebellion supported by Germany and Italy, even to the extent of standing by the legal right to supply the Spanish government with arms, we shall get the country into the war. We must keep it out, which we can do by making a bargain on the lines that if our soil is respected, if there are no bombs on our cities, we will surrender the ancient claims we have maintained in the past in respect to Spain and the Mediterranean route; and undertake not to intervene."

There followed, as we know, the nonintervention committee—"nonintervention" meaning, as all the world is aware, that great Italian armies and armies of German technicians and great quantities of German material and planes and tanks should be allowed to destroy the Spanish government and Germany permitted to bring the whole peninsula within her effective control, establishing herself in a strategic position so powerful that it may prove a very great factor in the defeat and destruction of the British Empire.

I have said above that that kind of bargain takes place when a nation has lost a clear sense, in its defensive activity, of what it is it should defend; what is indispensable to defense; what defense *is*.

So confused had this sense become in certain

circles in Britain, that in the Press, in the House of Commons, there was repeatedly great jubilation when Germany and Italy secured victories in their Spanish campaign, though the purpose, the obvious and even avowed purpose, of that campaign was the reduction of the British Empire to impotence. Yet those who thus rejoiced belonged to the Imperialist group; whom a critic might call the Professional Patriots; hostile to all things foreign; to the last man of them in favor of ever-increasing armaments; and all ready to "lay down their lives for the defense of the country." Some of them have so died.

They were guilty of strange contradictions just outlined owing to confusions born of certain violent prejudices, partisanships, partly political, partly social, partly economic, even partly religious. What they invoked as justification for their hatred of the Spanish government was quite often largely true. That government, or parties supporting it, had at times been oppressive, guilty of great cruelties—much as is the present Spanish government. But the violence of their feelings was often due to their refusal to see other facts. In any case their prejudices and partisanships obscured the real issues of defense, which are at bottom simple enough.

About the story, one or two outstanding features should be noted. The first is this: There came a point when the whole policy of submission to the course of German policy broke down and the British attitude was completely changed; principles which had been repudiated and derided for years were suddenly recognized as inevitable, and adopted. If the truths which were accepted late had been accepted early, there would have been no war. "If," said one commentator, "we had been prepared in time to say that we *would* do, what at long last we were in any case compelled to do, we should not have had to do it."

The second feature is this: Exactly the same kind of divisions and conflicts of opinion, the same confusions born of the same prejudices and partisanships obscuring the conditions of effective national defense, exist in this country. The actors have different names but the roles are the same. Where "Russian propaganda" served as a bogey which deprived many Englishmen of sound judgment, talk of "British propaganda" does that same service for some Americans. There is indeed an almost comic parallelism between the attitude of certain powerful sections in America today and powerful sections of the British public a year or two since; the same prolonged refusal to recognize certain principles of policy and then a sudden adoption of them when the country faces mortal peril and when perhaps it is too late for the policy, which earlier would have saved the situation, to be applied at all.

And a third feature is the bearing of the story on two guiding principles of Hitler's policy. The two main lines have been indicated clearly in two of his statements. The first of them is this:

> Our strategy is to destroy the enemy from within, to conquer him through himself.

And the second is this:

> A clever conqueror will always, if possible, impose his demands on the conquered by installments. For a people that makes a voluntary surrender saps its own character; and with such a people you can calculate, that none of these oppressions in detail will supply quite enough reason for it to resort once more to arms. The more such extortions are suffered without re-

sistance, the more unjustifiable it comes to seem to people to make any ultimate stand against pressures which appear each to be new and isolated, though in fact there is perpetual recurrence of them.

They are the basis of Hitler's military successes.

Let us see how they might be applied to America.

Chapter IV

THE EVENT ANSWERS
THE ISOLATIONIST

The facts and history of the naval position. The nature of the Hitlerian strategy: to divide and "turn" the power that he faces. How Hitler does it. The method in the United States. The case of France. The world situation if Britain fails. The technique of assault upon America.

The reader will agree, perhaps, that the second chapter of this book embodies a fairly comprehensive statement of the case for American isolationism. The statement has been based, with all the fairness and detachment which this writer could summon to the task, upon presentations of that case made by its most outstanding, most competent, most sincere and respected advocates using indeed, for the most part, their own form of presentation.

There is one feature of the case which stands apart from its other aspects and which can be disposed of at the beginning: the relation of the British fleet to the defensive preparations of the country now being feverishly hastened.

No very technical knowledge is necessary in order to recognize the realities of the naval position.

Men of all opinions—including, and particularly, some of the extremest of the isolationists in and out of Congress—are demanding the creation of a two-ocean navy for America on the assumption that attack may come both in the Pacific and the Atlantic; and may come simultaneously. If that danger is not real then the demand for a vast increase in the American navy is indeed "hysteria," the condition with which Colonel Lindbergh assures us the country is now stricken in its fears of Nazi power. The isolationist, far from attributing the demands for a two-ocean navy to "hysteria," insists that it is based upon a most vital need, and the greatest possible danger.

So be it. But please note:

The new navy cannot by any possibility be built before 1946.[1]

---

[1] The report of the Senate Committee on Naval Affairs.

We are concerned therefore mainly to know what may happen during those six years.

To those who insist, as does Mr. Upton Close, that the British navy does not serve as any defense to this country, never has done so, is never likely to do so, and its existence is indeed the main menace against which this country has to provide—to those who support such propositions, one or two very simple questions might profitably be put.

If the British navy were sunk or captured by the Axis powers next week—by Japan operating in the Far East, Italy in the Mediterranean and Germany in the Atlantic—would the danger, which all isolationists agree exists and can only be remedied six years hence—would that danger be brought nearer by the disappearance of the British fleet or be rendered more remote? Would the country be less in danger if the British fleet no longer existed?

Now there is only one honest answer to that question. The whole of America knows that with the disappearance of the British fleet that danger (against which America is now providing by a new fleet which cannot exist until 1946) would become instantly much more acute.

Then it is obvious that the British fleet *does* in some measure serve as a protection to the United States. And in that case, what is the meaning of the rhetorical flourishes indulged in by Mr. Close about the "absurdity" of the idea that the British fleet protects any American interest?

It is, I think, Mr. Lippmann who has pointed out that Senator Walsh, who presided over the Senate Naval Committee which approved the "two-ocean navy" legislation and knows it will not exist for at least six years, is firmly convinced that if America takes the risks of helping the British navy to continue to exist, she will be in greater danger than if she took the risk of letting the British navy be sunk or captured.

Moreover, the historical citations by which it is sought to prove that the British fleet has never protected any American interest, or has always been the main menace to the United States and about the only thing against which this country has had to protect itself and the rest of it, is surely very "selective" history indeed.

The truth is that common action by Britain and America in resistance to the menace of European combinations against this country has been a feature of America's policy during considerably more than a hundred years. A President of the United States writes the following:

> With the British power and navy combined with our own, we have nothing to fear from the rest of the world; and in the great struggle of the epoch between liberty and despotism, we owe it to ourselves to sustain the former, in this hemisphere at least.

That might have been written in the year 1940. As a matter of fact it was written a hundred and seventeen years ago by James Madison, who had actually as President led the nation against Britain in the War of 1812. Postwar conditions had persuaded him that only co-operation between the United States and Britain could prevent the expansion of Europe's more reactionary powers into the New World.

Mr. Close is certain that it is contrary to all America's tradition to regard the British navy as any part of American defense. Well, after Madison, one might cite one of the authors of the Declaration of Independence as pretty good authority for "American tradition." The facts ought to be known (but it would seem are not by some who write of America's traditions), as Walter Lippmann has recently recalled them.

ALONE *OR* ALLIED?

In 1823 the victorious Holy Alliance was threatening to reconquer the Spanish colonies in this hemisphere which had recently proclaimed their independence. Simultaneously, to the west, Russia was threatening to extend its power from Alaska down the Pacific Coast. Then, as now, this hemisphere was threatened on both sides by a coalition of victorious imperial states, and it was under those conditions that President Monroe, acting through the American Minister in London, entered into negotiations with Canning, the British Foreign Secretary. The negotiations began in August, 1823, and the results reached Washington on October 9, 1823. They provided for some kind of joint American and British policy to forbid the Holy Alliance to enter this hemisphere.

President Monroe sent the documents to Jefferson, who studied them for a week and replied that, while "America, North and South, have a set of interests distinct from those of Europe, and particularly her own" there is "one nation" which "could disturb us in this purpose; she now offers to lead, aid and accompany us in it. By acceding to her proposition, we detach her from the bonds, bring her mighty weight into the scale of free government, and emancipate a continent at one stroke, which might otherwise linger long in doubt and difficulty." Supported by Jefferson's approval, President Monroe, in a message to Congress on December 2, 1823, proclaimed the Monroe Doctrine.

A very precise account of the events which led up to and followed the proclamation of the Monroe Doctrine is given in a speech of Calhoun's in 1848 delivered just after the popular movement of that time had seen the end of the despotic governments against whose policy the Monroe Doctrine was directed. Speaking of the circumstances which led to the establishment of the Doctrine, Calhoun said:

> The Allied powers were the four great continental monarchies—Russia, Prussia, Austria, and France. Shortly after the overthrow of Bonaparte these powers entered into an alliance called the "Holy Alliance," the object of which was to sustain and extend the monarchical principles as far as possible, and to oppress and put down popular institutions. England, in the early stages of the alliance, favored it. The members of the alliance held several congresses, attended either by themselves or their ambassadors, and

undertook to regulate the affairs of all Europe, and actually interfered in the affairs of Spain for the purpose of putting down popular doctrines.

In its progress the alliance turned its eyes to this continent, in order to aid Spain in regaining her sovereignty over her revolted provinces. At this stage England became alarmed. Mr. Canning was then Prime Minister. He informed Mr. Rush (the American minister in London) of the project, and gave to him at the same time the assurance that, if sustained by the United States, Great Britain would resist. Mr. Rush immediately communicated this to our government. It was received here with joy; for so great was the power of the alliance that even we did not feel ourselves safe from its interpositions. Indeed, it was anticipated, almost as a certain result, that if the interference took place with the governments of South America, the alliance would ultimately extend its interference to ourselves.

I remember the reception of the despatch from Mr. Rush as distinctly as if all the circumstances had occurred yesterday. I well recollect the great satisfaction with which it was received by the Cabinet. It came late in the year, not long before the meeting of Congress. As was usual with Mr. Monroe upon great occasions, the papers were sent round to each member of the Cabinet, so that each might be duly apprised of all the circumstances, and be prepared to give his opinion. The Cabinet met. It deliberated. There was long and careful consultation; and the result was the declaration which I have just announced.

All this has passed away. That very movement on the part of England, sustained by this declaration, gave a blow to the celebrated alliance from which it never recovered. From that time forward it gradually decayed, till it utterly perished. The late revolutions in Europe have put an end to all its work, and nothing remains of all that it ever did.

------- ❁ -------

Certain questions are raised by the Monroe Doctrine.

The main argument of this book is the need, if what remains of a free world is to be saved, of a policy of common action against aggression.

For 120 years America has formally recognized the need of that element in its foreign policy, for the Monroe Doctrine is, of course, a partial expression for that belief: "an attack on one is an attack on all." Monroe's proclamation said in effect: "If you touch one American republic, you touch us." And since his time attempts have been made to widen the principle of

70

that doctrine by making it reciprocal; securing, as at Havana, common action of all American republics in the face of certain forms of aggression.

This is in accordance with the principle for which this book pleads.

But note a strange anomaly.

The most extreme of the isolationists is prepared to plunge America into war, to have American boys die on foreign soil, if Patagonia is attacked by an overseas power. But on what grounds of strategy, or sense, is the isolationist prepared to have American boys die on foreign soil in order to prevent the German occupation of Patagonia, but will not move a finger in order to prevent the German occupation of Ireland? Is it that Ireland is so much farther away than Patagonia? But Ireland is much nearer. Is it that the preservation of Latin-American democracy from domination by dictators is much more vital to America than the preservation of democracy in Ireland, or Wales, or England? But many Latin-American republics are plain dictatorships already, always have been, and do not really pretend to be anything else.

Would the defeat of, say, the Argentinian or Brazilian navy be more menacing to America than the destruction or capture of the British navy? There is no Latin-American navy whose defeat would seriously upset the balance of sea power in the world. The destruction or capture of the British navy would do so to the extent of putting this country in mortal peril. So one asks: Why do the isolationists declare that, though Britain perish, we should not move a ship to save her, but announce that if Patagonia is in peril, our boys will die to defend her?

IN WHICH DIRECTION WILL THE GUNS SHOOT?

Let us now return to a consideration of the isolationist position in its more general aspect.

The central proposition of the case or outline in Chapter II is that this country, by reason of its extent and vast material resources, is impregnable, if not invulnerable, so long as its power is devoted mainly to the defense of its soil, or the soil of the Western Hemisphere, and is not dissipated by participation in the disputes of other nations, the interminable quarrels of Europe.

In support of this is invoked the past experience of the country in the face of enemy attack; as past experience—particularly the experience of the aftermath of the last World War—is also invoked as proof of the uselessness of this country's attempting to take sides in foreign disputes since their complexity makes it in practice impossible for America to control the course of events in which she would be involved.

As against that case, I submit the following proposition:

If American power is limited to the defense of American soil, and if Britain is defeated, the American people will be brought under the subjugation of Nazi power about as completely as Scandinavia, the Low Countries, Czechoslovakia, Austria, France, and the countries of the Balkans have been brought. That result may, in America's case, be achieved virtually without war (as it was in the case of Austria, of Czechoslovakia, of Norway, of Sweden, of Denmark, of Holland, of Roumania, of Hungary, of Bulgaria), with the armaments of the country becoming part of the instrument by which a minority, co-operating with the Nazi power, enforced the New Order on the majority; or the result may be achieved

73

after some resistance, as in the case of Poland, Belgium, France; or after fierce resistance like that which Britain is now opposing. But with the destruction of the British Empire and the passing of the rest of the world under complete Axis (i.e., Nazi) domination, the submergence of the existing American way of life under the rising tide of the new forces would, in the light of unmistakable experience, be, humanly speaking, quite certain.

It is irrelevant to that proposition to go on citing the extent of America's material resources, her capacity for the production of arms, her aptitude for mechanization, or even her invulnerability to invasion in the face of well-defended coasts and a modern navy. For what America has to face mainly is not frontal attack upon those forces, so much as their "turning" in a more than military sense; the possibility that they may be diverted from their original purpose of resisting the revolutionary movement now sweeping over the world, into becoming instruments of that movement. This reversal of the purpose of national power will be achieved by broadly the same technique which Hitler has so repeatedly and so successfully employed against the forces of the European continent, forces in sum total enormously greater than his own; a technique not primarily military at all, but political, moral, psychological; only at a second stage military.

TO DIVIDE AND TURN

Those who doubt the possibility of this technique being applied to America have overlooked the revolutionary—or, if you will, counter-revolutionary—character of the present World War; the fact that, in every case where the Nazi power has moved against a country, there are interests in that country—political, economic or personal —which would be better served (or, what usually comes to the same thing so far as the event is concerned) would appear to be better served by Nazi victory than by Nazi defeat. Those interests need not for the purposes of Nazi technique be very widespread, if, in a time of confusion and cross-purposes, they can be helped to the seizure of strategically important political positions.

Hitler has demonstrated, again and again, that by this non-military technique, arms built up for the purpose of resisting him can, not merely be removed from his path—often without battle at all as in the case of the magnificent military equipment of Czechoslovakia—but be used as an instrument for the further subjugation of the very people who have created them. He has shown that this same technique can be so employed as to bring an ancient and age-long opponent over from the ranks of the enemy to his own as in some degree France has been brought, so that within the space of a little over a month, ships which had been in effect part of the British navy were being used to fight that navy, sink its ships and kill its sailors. (A few days before these lines were written a further naval engagement took place between French and British forces. *French* planes were bombing Gibraltar and, at the moment of writing, the French government is seriously considering the proposal of formally declaring war upon Great Britain, of becoming, that is, one of the Axis powers bent upon her destruction.)

Such an outcome of forty years of entente or alliance with Britain was made possible only by the development within France of certain political and moral forces, a certain group of ideas, the military importance of which the Germans recognized far more clearly than did the British. For years, practically in the sight of the whole world, Germany had been busy developing those forces, forces which were not regarded by the British as having any military or naval significance. What interested the British admiralty for instance—and what was often being discussed— was the technical quality of the French fleet, or its enlargement. But the question that someone should have been asking was: "Of what avail the improved power of the French fleet if its ultimate destiny is to be used against us?"[2]

Hitler has done something more than "turn"

[2] Five years ago a series of articles contributed by this present writer to the London *Daily Telegraph* began thus:

"An Empire's security depends, obviously, at least as much upon its political situation in the world—that is, upon the answer to the question: 'Who, when the guns begin to go off, will be on its side and who against it?'—as upon its military and naval resources.

"Yet there is a curious tendency to evade this plain fact. About some alleged shortage of planes or shells, or a given type of cruiser, it is easy to stir widespread public interest. But a change in the international situation which may mean that whole armies and navies are shifting over from the side of our defence to the side of potential aggression leaves the same public relatively indifferent."

An English observer at a Washington Naval Conference remarked during a rather weary discussion of gun calibres: "I am less interested in the calibre of these guns than in the direction in which ultimately they will shoot. Will it be at us or at a common enemy? It makes a difference."

the lines opposing him: he has taken over the resources which they were planned to defend, in order to add them to his own power.

The details of the method are not obscure. Hitler has often described it for all the world to hear, if they so cared. (It is indicative of his contempt for the general intelligence that he quite freely discusses in talk and writing precisely how he proposes to proceed.) That technique is based, first of all, upon the oldest and most hackneyed device of tyranny—Divide and Rule—applied, however, with a far-reaching thoroughness that only modern technology could make possible.

He has never objected to his enemies arming; what he has forbidden with all the hidden forces at his command is their co-operation to resist him. He has said in effect:

Not only will we divide the non-German world in the sense of preventing any combination of non-German nations against us by playing upon nationalist separatism and isolationism so that we can destroy them all in detail, picking them off one by one; we will render powerful countries like France and America impotent by internal divisions. To render a country impotent to resist us, we don't have to make the whole of its people favorable to us or for that matter any of its people. We have only to persuade a section that our triumph is a lesser evil than the things involved in resistance to us, a lesser evil than certain other things they fear; that, for instance, a German-dominated Europe will be less dangerous for them than a Communist Europe; that our defeat will mean the triumph of Communist Russia. Indeed, we do not even have to achieve that conviction, only doubts about it, creating such indecisions that steps indispensable to any effective resistance are put off so late that finally it is impossible to take them and the initiative is left to us.

Having by the manipulation of ideas—of prejudices, hates, confusions—divided his enemies so that he could take them one by one, he made the subjugation of the less powerful a means by which the more powerful could be outflanked and encircled. He did not proceed against France or Britain until a very large measure of strategic encirclement had been accomplished by the acquisition of Austria (accomplished by an internal disruption operated through the local Nazis, aided from outside); by the domination of the Spanish peninsula through a more indirect method, aid extended to a satellite state undertaking actual invasion; by the reoccupation of the Rhineland, achieved when those who should have resisted had their attention diverted elsewhere and were quarreling among themselves; by the conquest of Czechoslovakia through a combination of the Austrian method plus bamboozlement of elderly French and British statesmen.

Two features are to be noted: Hitler did not create the elements of confusion, disruption, disintegration of which he availed himself; he manipulated them. Their origins went, of course, far beyond the period of the Austrian or the Rhineland business; back beyond the Italian-Abyssinian episode; beyond the Japanese-Manchurian, to the confusions which just after the peace caused America to drop out of the tripartite British-French-American undertaking to resist in common any return of German aggression; and later caused Britain to do likewise.

But the second and much more astonishing feature of the story is that although the process by which the West was being undermined, disintegrated, encircled, went on quite visibly, and Hitler wrote and talked about it and shouted his intentions from the housetops, the governments and the publics of the Western nations paid no real attention. They went on with their little internecine quarrels and bickerings; the personal intrigues of party politics, each Western nation quite convinced apparently that these world-wide processes, the threat of deep upheavals spreading so rapidly from Manchuria to Africa, from Africa to Central Europe, from Central Europe to the Rhineland, from the Rhineland to Spain—that this could not possibly concern them, or reach them.

For some reason or other it was impossible to get adequate attention to the thing either from the public or from public men. They often professed to know all about it; many professed "inside knowledge." Quite clearly the meaning of it all escaped them.

It would be quite useless to indicate how the technique involved might be applied to the United States unless there is understanding, clearer than seems until yesterday, to have existed in England, for instance, of the way in which the technique has already been applied in the Old World; an understanding of what really explains the fact that seventy millions have within a few months subjugated some two hundred millions and will, if Britain falls, bring a thousand million within their power.

Before, therefore, undertaking an outline (which will be done presently) of the way in which the Hitlerian method might be applied to the United States, let us take a somewhat closer look at its method in Europe, especially in view of the fact that with all our talk of Fifth Columns and Trojan horses we are obviously still mistaking both their habitat and their habits.

HOW HITLER DOES IT

It is one of the curious facts about this tragedy that an illiterate house painter has understood the overwhelming military importance of ideas far more clearly than most of the rulers who have preceded him. So often those who make up governments, and particularly perhaps soldiers and military leaders responsible for defense, take the line: "Ideas, ideals, opinions, theories, don't matter. It is only power, force, guns, planes, ships that count." Hitler has always known so much better than that and known that such a notion implies an almost childish confusion of thought. He knows that while nothing can be done without guns, the answer to the question who will get the guns and in which direction will they shoot, depends upon which idea prevails as against other ideas.

When Hitler started in Germany he had no power—no army, no guns, nothing; his party consisted of a baker's dozen of obscure agitators.

Throughout Hitler has realized far more clearly than his enemies that if you can direct a man's ideas you can direct his actions; that if you can determine what a man shall think and feel, you can determine what he shall do. He knew that if he was to get power and arms he could only do it by getting first of all at the minds of a certain number of his countrymen; putting ideas into the heads of a certain number of Germans, who in their turn would put the ideas into other German heads. By working upon people's sense of grievance, disappointments, tempers, resentments, hates, the readiness of men to blame their misfortunes upon anything but their own failings and mistakes, his party grew. He could not use force at this stage: again, he had none. But he was using the kind of persuasion of which he is master, demagogy of a particularly mean and evil kind, to get force. The ideas had to come before force. Having, by the method of persuasion, propaganda, expanded his party from thirteen persons to several millions and made it master of Germany, he then proceeded, by exactly the same technique, to make Germany master of Europe, as a preliminary stage to making her master of the world.

If Hitler really believed that ideas were unimportant and only arms counted, why did he establish the greatest, the most elaborate, the most expensive machine for the dissemination and control of ideas that the world has ever seen?

He knew that a relatively small but united minority, knowing what it wants, prepared to be ruthless, can dominate a much greater majority, that is divided as to what it wants, so that one part of it can be played off against another part and to the whole applied the principle of "Divide and Rule." He knew that non-German Europe had infinitely more power than Germany, and that if the non-German world were really united against him, he would be impotent. But he knew also that non-German Europe was not united and that he could play upon national animosities to dominate the whole. Again, it did not matter to him how much nations armed against him, if only each would remain isolationist—which, alas, they were only too ready to do. What could a Norway do, however heavily it armed, or a Denmark, or a Holland, or even a France, so long as it did not combine with others? From the moment that each said: "We will fight for ourselves alone; only when the invader attacks *us*"—from that moment they were all at his mercy: he could destroy them in detail.

One of the first tasks, therefore, of his vast propaganda machine was to sustain and inflame the idea of nationalist isolationism. He said in effect to other nations: "You can arm all you like but if you make combinations, you will know my wrath." And it worked. The Scandinavian states dare not combine, nor the Low Countries, for fear that Hitler would regard such combinations as an unfriendly act. Even when the invader was almost on the doorstep of the Low Countries they dared not take precautionary measures of co-operation with others. And of course their timidities, the fearful care which they took not to offend him, their scrupulous regard for all the minutiae of "neutrality" did not deter him one fraction of a second, or deflect his course the fraction of an inch the moment that it became convenient for his purpose to fall upon them and destroy them.

It was not difficult to arrange that there should be no unified resistance to him among those he intended to destroy. His greatest success in that respect was, of course, to separate Russia from the Western democracies. By years of violent vituperation and invective leveled at Russia as the one nation in the world with which he could never co-operate or even make peace (for several years that kind of statement entered into every speech that Hitler made) he persuaded the bourgeoisie of the West that he stood as their protector against impending Bolshevist revolution and ruin. Having thus succeeded in separating Russia from the West, he promptly proceeded to make an ally of this same Russia. He had brought the power of the greatest nation of the Old World over from the side of the West to his own side, by a form of propaganda no more secret and elusive than violent tirades delivered in the Sportspalast in Berlin.

And just as he succeeded in preventing the co-operation of the lesser states, and of the greater Western democracies with Russia, he finally succeeded in the separation of France from Britain. One recalls the slogans which even before the war were heard a little everywhere in France: "France is being dragged into Britain's war"; "France is being asked to pull the British chestnuts out of the fire"; "France is being used to enable Britain to keep her ill-gotten possessions"; "Britain will fight to the last Frenchman."

The seeds so sown grew sufficiently not, it is true, to prevent common action by France and Britain in 1939, but sufficiently to create and keep alive a strong and anti-English party in France which at the moment of strain gained the upper hand and pushed France, not only to a separate peace, but what has been even more disastrous, a peace which for a time makes France the virtual ally of Germany against Britain.

And just as he succeeded by a mixture of propaganda and terror in separating one nation from another in any resistance to him, he succeeded by the same means in dividing each nation within itself. He kept before himself constantly that watchword: "Our strategy is to destroy the enemy from within, to conquer him through himself." And we know by what technique of "cells" within every nation of the world the principle has been applied. He knew he did not need to convert majorities to his cause; a very small minority —perhaps a two or three per cent, as in the case of Norway; a five or six per cent in the case of Denmark; about the same proportion perhaps in the case of Belgium (taking care that the percentage included some of the entourage of the King) were sufficient to create the necessary hesitations at the right moment.

We have seen how all this has worked out in the case of France, and is being tried so energetically in the United States. In the case of France Hitler exploited first of all the distrust of Russia. He utilized all the forces of his vast propaganda machine to intensify the fears which a bourgeois people naturally held of Communism, and of Russia as the source of Communism, although he knew that he himself would be quite ready when the time came to make a bargain with Russia;

knew that he would not in the least be deterred by
the fears with which he managed to frighten
France. (And parenthetically the question we
have to answer in respect of Russia is not which
of the two systems, the Nazi and the Communist,
is the more evil within their respective countries
—the Communist may be the more evil and bar-
barous—but which is the more dangerous exter-
nally, outside those countries. And of that there
can hardly be much doubt. It is not Russian forces
which have overrun the ancient civilized Atlantic
democracies, using their territories as bases for
attack upon the remaining democracies. Russia
could never have done it.)

And you know also that the slogans which became so common in France and elsewhere were
followed up by things more active: subversive
Fascist groups were subsidized with money, provided with arms; to young men from the universities was held out the prospect that if they played
their cards properly they might become the governing element of their country; that it would be
placed in their charge; that they would become
kings, possessors of great powers wherewith they
could regenerate their fatherland (to say nothing

of enriching themselves) ; purging her of foreign influences from across the Channel, liberating her from the Jews and the financiers, the Socialists and the internationalists. While the bourgeoisie and property owners were assured that a triumphant Germany would protect them from Communism, the workers were told that Germany was after all, out to destroy capitalism, that that destruction might provide an opportunity for the coming of Socialism; that indeed Germany stood for the right kind of Socialism.

And let us face all the truth: What Germany was doing in France to create hostility to Britain, she was also doing in Britain to create hostility to France, and in Belgium hostility to France and Britain alike; and succeeding—again not sufficiently to cause King Leopold crudely to sell out to Germany but sufficiently to cause him to hesitate to make effective arrangements beforehand with Britain and France for the defense of Belgium; and those hesitations finally brought about the surrender of a Belgian army of half a million men opening the road to Dunkerque and the encirclement of a Franco-British army of three-quarters of a million.

ALONE *OR* ALLIED?

THE METHOD IN THE UNITED STATES

Exactly the same technique is operating before our eyes in the United States. The German machine does not even try to win over America to the German cause, or to convince the public as a whole that German triumph would be good for America, something America ought to aid. Dr. Goebbels knows his business well enough to realize that such an effort could only help to defeat Germany's purpose. For America would react violently against it. And it is not in the least necessary at this stage from the German point of view. It will suffice to apply to the United States some of the technique applied so successfully to France: make no effort to create an opinion favorable to Germany but make every effort to create an opinion if not unfavorable then lukewarm to Britain and keep alive the idea that it is a struggle of rival European nations. Keep alive the old doubts about Britain. See that the old slogans are kept in circulation. This is Britain's war; America has no concern in it; it has come about because, as Lindbergh puts it, "Britain has got too much of the earth and Germany too little," and

America is being asked to help Britain retain the spoils of old piracies. These suggestions do not need to be entirely successful. If they create some doubts, some indecisions, some delays, so that America, in her heart of hearts knowing that Britain fights her battle, nevertheless aids that battle "too little and too late," that will suffice for Germany's purpose.

Only at a later stage will it be necessary for the Fifth Column to take the lead.

The worst Fifth Column danger does not lie in the Bund, in the quarters so carefully investigated by the Dies Committee, but in the confused thinking, the oscillations of judgment of great masses of the public, represented very often by sincere, patriotic, high-minded and highly placed personages, men as high-minded and sincere as King Leopold himself; as Weygand, Pétain and other members of the Vichy government, now so pathetically and helplessly the tools of the Nazi power.

But before the "Vichy" stage is reached must come the stage of the Chamberlains and the Daladiers, the Simons and the Bonnets, the Hoares and the Lavals; of men who, with the best intentions in the world, particularly with the intention, consistently followed, of avoiding war, bring their country at last to a strategic position such that it is unable effectively to repel the blows of the enemy when he decides that it is time to strike.

For note one detail of the Hitler strategy. It was plainly *not* his intention to precipitate war with Britain or France until he had put them in a strategic position which would render them impotent. He had hoped that after the bloodless absorption of Austria and Czechoslovakia, and the reduction of Spain to a puppet state, Poland would have been absorbed as bloodlessly; and from thence he would have gone on to the bloodless acquisition of Scandinavia and the Low Countries, with their navies, shipping and air bases, thus completing the strategic encirclement of France and Britain. He had seen Britain retreat before Japan in the Far East, before Italy in the Eastern Mediterranean, before German-Italian threats in the Eastern Mediterranean, before Germany in the Rhineland. When Britain and France called a halt, at the stage of Poland, he still followed broadly his previous technique. The Finnish incident proved that the "Oslo" states—Norway, Sweden, Denmark, Belgium, Holland—would neither unite nor allow Britain or France to make defensive arrangements with them, so that it would still be easy to pick them off one by one. Until he had made this certain he arranged for the war to be "peaceful," a "sitz-krieg," a "phony" war. The six months of sitz-krieg enabled Germany to go on with her preparations for the seizure of Scandinavia and the Low Countries much as she would have done if "war" had not been declared in September. When the Oslo powers were at his mercy and he could operate from the Norwegian, Danish and Dutch bases, the real war began.

Watching the steady dissolution of non-German Europe, especially when marked by such incidents as the defection of Leopold, the part played by the Quislings—the little local Nazi leaders—of Norway, Denmark, Holland, Belgium, France; the piecemeal character of the conquests, "one at a time," we understand what prompted Hitler to write that his strategy was to destroy the enemy from within, "to conquer him through himself" and to secure "surrender by installments," profiting by the psychological truth that each surrender makes the next seem more reasonable until power of resistance has disappeared.

THE CASE OF FRANCE

Since the collapse of France there have appeared in this country as elsewhere innumerable explanations of that tragedy. As one who himself lived nearly twenty years in France and has known many of the personalities involved, I would say that the briefest and fairest of the many postmortems is that contained in one of Commander King-Hall's News Letters coming from a source which has truly "inside knowledge."

In his report this particular writer places in the very forefront of the forces which explain the collapse of Europe the precise fact emphasized in the foregoing analysis: the factor of "ideas," confusion as to what really it is all about; whether resistance may not bring more real disaster than would submission. It is this factor which explains why "the French Army was never concentrated, that there was never a real big battle and that the weapon with which Hitler has defeated the French Republic was not the armored vehicle and the dive bomber, but that invisible and deadly weapon 'ideas'—the real revelation of this war."

Just as Austria and Czechoslovakia, Poland and Norway, Holland and Belgium were corrupted, so was France completely undermined by this invisible weapon of the Germans, and the country was more than 50 per cent conquered before the first German tank crossed the bridge on the Meuse, which the retreating French Army incidentally forgot to blow up.

Nobody can be surprised except those who were determined in all circumstances to keep their eyes closed to what was going on. Years ago Hitler told Rauschning quite clearly that whenever he started military action, he would make quite certain by appropriate propaganda offensives in advance, that his troops would be received without the will to resist. I do urge every Briton who has not yet read Rauschning's *Hitler Speaks,* to do so now, and if possible to learn by heart those pages which tell of Hitler's methods of warfare, foreign policy and propaganda.

When a new Shakespeare one day arises to tell the story of the intrigues of Paul Reynaud's most intimate entourage, of the diabolical influence of Madame de Portes and her friends Baudouin, Prouvost and others, of the unlimited personal ambitions of General Weygand who, when he realised that he could not become another Foch, decided at least to remain master in defeat, of the sinister role played by the old Marshal Pétain, who did not understand anything of the tactics of the young German generals (Hitler has particularly good luck with Marshals over eighty), then mankind will see unfolded a drama as unprecedented as it is unbelievable.

It is of vital importance to the British people to understand the methods by which Hitler has conquered the European countries one by one. Each of them, like the small animal hypnotised by a serpent, was unable to use its muscles at the moment when the beast opened its mouth. We are witnessing a revolution which we still do not understand. All the notions regarding international relations, all the rules of diplomacy and warfare, all our theories concerning nation, people, religion, sovereignty, rights have been overthrown by the Nazi conception. We went down into the arena in a snow white dress to play a thrilling game of tennis. But the other fellow over the net is playing catch-as-catch-can.

What are the main arguments by which Nazi propaganda is obtaining such amazing results? Naturally they vary in every country, just as in Germany before he got to power, Hitler promised everything to everybody. But the basic microbe of disease is the following thesis:

AMERICA'S DILEMMA:

Social upheavals are menacing the ruling classes everywhere, and the only defence against such communistic and socialistic movements is a dictatorship of the Nazi or Fascist type. It is true that even ministers, industrial leaders and bankers must give up in a totalitarian regime parts of their personal freedom, but instead of that they have the powerful defence of a totalitarian regime to maintain their social and material situation.

I have heard many leading people in France arguing during the last days which preceded the capitulation—and which were probably the last days of the Third Republic—that the national principle is dead, that it is all the same whether there are French soldiers or German soldiers in the country, the main thing is that there should be "Order." Even General Weygand, in the dramatic meeting of the Cabinet at Tours, emphasized the necessity of ending hostilities, arguing that "at least one part of the army must be saved for maintaining order." It was at this Cabinet meeting that M. Mandel bitterly asked Pétain and Weygand, how it was that they were now preaching defeatism when they had been brought into the Cabinet to fight on to victory.

So it is obvious that what happened at Tours and at Bordeaux was a real coup d'etat, with the will to end hostilities with Germany and Italy, and not the consequence of a defeat of the French Army in the field. This coup d'etat means not only the end of hostilities, but also the end of the constitutional regime in France, for the Pétain Government is constituted in the majority of generals and non-parliamentarians, and it has never received a vote of confidence in Parliament.

This makes it clear why the Fleet and Air Force were not sent, before the request for an armistice, to England or to the French Colonies: those who are responsible for this coup d'etat wanted complete surrender to Germany and Italy in order to establish a Fascist regime in France and they are frightened of a continuance of the war by Britain, believing that any prolongation of hostilities might end in the dreaded social revolution.

This will to surrender to the Nazi and Fascist regimes is nothing new in history. It has too often been the case that defeated nations have adopted the political system of their conquerors. In 1918, the democratic elements were working on the defeat of Imperial Germany, and after the Allied victory they established an even more democratic regime than we had in France and in England. Now we are witnessing the manifestation of the same historical law in the reverse direction.

It cannot be emphasized strongly enough how important it is that Britons should not merely smile at these happenings, just as did the Czechs, the Poles, the Danes, the Norwegians, the Belgians, the Dutch and the French saying: "It can't happen here." It happened everywhere and it *can* happen here also. And it almost certainly will happen here unless the British Government and the British people realise that this invisible weapon is at least as dangerous as the German air fleet and mechanised divisions, unless we decide to wage war on that field with the greatest vigour, unless we give up our defensive attitude and go out with the flame and the religious persuasion of the Crusaders in our hearts, to conquer the world for our ideas.

IF BRITAIN FALLS

Let us see how, once Great Britain has been overcome, the Nazi method properly adapted could be applied to the United States.

The preliminary condition of the whole outline or forecast, namely the defeat of Britain and the circumstances which would follow that event, is difficult to keep in mind because difficult to imagine. But the happening of unimaginable things has become exceedingly commonplace this last twelve months and somehow we must manage to picture these contigencies or we cannot make our decision between course of action at all.

ALONE *OR* ALLIED?

If London, Manchester and the main ports are, by a bombardment continued unremittingly for many months, at last really reduced to ruin so that the water, sewage, light, power, gas and communications are put out of order; the population by sheer physical exhaustion, lack of sleep, by illness, and epidemic reduced to stupefaction; the sense of national direction by that fact impaired or lost, there would arise, necessarily, a "Vichy" government making the best terms it could with Hitler. These terms would, of course, include the passing under the power of the Axis of the whole of the British Empire with (for the time being) the single exception of that part of it in North America.

There would thus pass under the directing control of Germany, as the hard core of its new empire, the whole of Europe from the Arctic Ocean to the Mediterranean, from Ireland to the Vistula; a territory whose population is immensely greater than that of the United States, with resources certainly not inferior. The British Isles alone, in area and population quite a tiny part of Europe, contain the industrial equipment, the ammunition plants, the shipbuilding facilities of the greatest navy, the greatest mercantile marine, the greatest foreign trade which any nation in history has ever possessed. These factors have carried the power of Britain to the uttermost ends of the earth; have enabled her to maintain for two centuries the domination of India (three hundred and fifty million people, not savage for the most part, but of ancient civilization); of Africa, including South Africa, the largest source of the world's gold supply, and having upon its western coast and adjacent islands points suitable as airplane bases, much nearer than any others in the Old World, to the New.

We should confront in Berlin, not the government of Germany, but the government of virtually the whole of Europe west of the Russian border, since Italy is in fact the vassal and instrument of the larger power and lesser states like Sweden or Switzerland, if still unincorporated, would be in no position to put any brake upon policies which Berlin might pursue.

THE TECHNIQUE OF ASSAULT UPON AMERICA

The technique already so amazingly successful could be applied to the United States along some such lines as these:

ALONE *OR* ALLIED?

I

There would in early stages be no frontal attack upon the United States; no attempt at invasion. There would be instead,

2

Strategic encirclement (following the European pattern) based first upon political and ideological—but very peaceful—penetration of Latin-American states both in South and Central America. Much of the ideological inspiration would come through Spain. It is clear that Hitler sees in Spain the cultural motherland of all but two of the Latin-American republics. Hitler has had for some time an elaborate "cultural treaty" with Franco under the terms of which German teachers are to be admitted to Spanish schools, the works of Rosenberg and other Nazi philosophers to be there taught. For Spain is not only one of the vital strategic points from which to encircle France, challenge Britain in the Atlantic and in the Mediterranean, but is also a valuable jumping-off place for the cultural "conquest" of Spanish America, for triumph in the struggle of ideas, success in which Hitler has always regarded as indispensable to successful policy and action. Spain would become an instrument of propaganda.

We can be sure, therefore, that the books, plays, films, newspapers, wireless, radio programs coming from the Spanish motherland to the new Spain of the Americas will have been duly planned in Berlin.

It will be extremely difficult for the United States, of foreign speech, Protestant predominance, foreignness of ways and thought, to attempt to counter this elusive Nazi penetration of Latin America.

3

Concurrently with this would go on a process of commercial conquest which it would be exceedingly difficult for the United States to counter. Hitler in command now not only of Europe, but of most of the British Empire outside of North America, would command the production of not far short of a thousand million souls capable, under German discipline and centralized direction, of an output not only far greater than that of the United States but much more capable of centralized manipulation. For instance, Germany would be able to offer to South American states manufactured goods—textiles, farm machinery, tractors, motorcars—at prices with which America not employing slave or semi-slave labor could not possibly compete, while prices would be offered for buying the primary products of South America which the United States could not equal. It is true that the German people would profit little. Indeed the operation commercially might be a heavy loss. But advantage for the German people would not be the purpose of the arrangement. The purpose would be to increase the forces of the Nazi world power entrenching themselves in the Americas.

4

This economic and commercial penetration would lead up naturally to the establishment of well-organized, influential, wealthy Nazi parties which in due course would rise to power, reaching government by the electoral method or, if well supported from outside, would seize power as the result of a revolutionary movement like that of Franco in Spain, which Germany was supporting even before the guns began to go off.

There would not be a country in Latin America that would not have either a powerful Nazi party with its Henlein, its Seyss-Inquart, or its Quisling or a revolutionary movement with its Franco supported from Berlin. Once having captured power, these Latin Fuehrers would desire to co-operate with Berlin, since they would all in lesser or greater degree need outside support—support in arms, credit, money, trade. And these Berlin would control. It is not to the interest of the Hitlerian authority that subsidiary Fascist or Nazi governments should be too well supported at home. That might make them independent of Berlin. If Franco in Spain had a united Spanish people behind him, he might be in a position to defy Hitler: to refuse use of Spanish ports and air bases. In the same way a certain amount of "Italian unrest" is, from Hitler's point of view, good for the proper discipline of Mussolini.

5

Having ensured the presence of a number of Franco or Quisling governments in Latin America, dependent upon his aid, Hitler would then proceed, of course, to see that they were adequately armed for their defense. The armies, and navies, the submarine and air forces, would all possess German technical advisers, German "instructors," just as the branches of the German commercial houses would naturally have very large German staffs. Particularly would commercial aviation be very highly developed. Berlin would now possess all the airports along the West African coasts, the nearest to the New World of any other airports in the Old. (From Natal in Brazil to Dakar in Africa is a distance less than that flown every night by bombers of the R.A.F. as a matter of routine.)

6

The fact that a dozen or fifteen South and Central American republics were thus beginning to occupy, in relation to the Nazi Power, a position not very different from that occupied at present[3] by Spain, would, of course, be extremely disturbing to certain sections in the United States. What could the United States do about it? Tell a dozen Latin-American republics that they had to

[3] October, 1940. For the presence of large numbers of German troops in Spain may any day now be revealed.

terminate extremely profitable trade relations with Europe when the United States would be in no position to offer bargains as good as those which could be offered by the master of a thousand million producers, whose wages and conditions of work he could autocratically fix from one day to another? Tell those countries that they must not develop their commercial aviation? Dictate to them just the number of German technicians they may employ for the development of their oil wells, rubber plantations or cotton farms? Or dictate how their elections should be conducted when ballots revealed (as they certainly would if the training of local Nazis had been as thorough as we can be sure it would be) majorities in favor of the Nazi party as overwhelming as was the vote for Hitler in Austria just before he took that country under his protection? Any attempt by the United States to interfere would arouse all the old fears, dislikes, misgivings of Latin America concerning "Yankee imperialism," the "colossus of the North." If there were interference or dictation of any kind the United States would find itself with a dozen Irelands on her hands.

But there would be still more compelling reasons for noninterference. Large and influential groups in the United States itself would be as much in favor of the South American Francos as were powerful and influential groups in Britain openly, clamantly, with demonstrations in the House of Commons, in favor of the Spanish Franco, notwithstanding that his campaign was supported by German-Italian material and forces (without which it could never have succeeded) with the plain and obvious intention of so dominating the Spanish peninsula that they would be in a position to cut Britain's life line in the Mediterranean, sever a vital artery of the Empire. Note that these groups in Britain were not neutral to the conquest of Spain by Germany; they were violent and passionate in their advocacy of it, of what events have proved to be the Nazi cause.

7

The groups which in America would favor Francos and Latin-American republics would have a far stronger case than ever the British "Friends of Franco Spain"[4] possessed, in justifi-

[4] The name of a British organization which included at least one member of the then British government.

cation of their strange course. Dictatorship is native to Spanish America; parliamentary government has never really worked. It would not be simply a question, as in the Spanish matter, of allowing a government to secure arms with which to defend itself, but a more intricate problem of stopping the peaceful and perfectly legal infiltration of "commercial agents," "army instructors," "commercial aviators" and most potent and elusive of all, ideas—ideas promoted by popular, well-produced, well-illustrated newspapers, deriving funds from the advertising contracts of the aforementioned aviation companies; or commercial banks. These newspapers would of course consistently support the cause of all the local Nazi candidates; and they would possess sufficient circulation and influence to raise hurricanes of protest if the United States showed any disposition to interfere in the internal politics of a Latin-American nation. And dictatorial government, especially if aided by German technicians, might quite truly in much of Latin America be the alternative to disorder, chaos, bloodshed, military tyranny masquerading as "democracy." That was the charge of the pro-Franco British against the

Republican government of Spain. Religious considerations entered, as did of course the fear of encouragement to Communism at home (this was particularly the case of France). In the mists and gales of passionate "crusades" German-Italian design was obscured, and the threat to the empire overlooked.

This would not be less the case when, with disorder arising in some Latin-American republic, with Communists and anarchists running amok, with churches being sacked, priests murdered, nuns raped, oil wells set on fire, foreigners killed, their property wantonly destroyed, a "party of law and order" should appear in that country, capture the government, impose order, hang the rapists, put the Communists and the anarchists under lock and key, open the churches, restore the property of the foreigners, protect their homes. Such a government in such circumstances would have the warm support of great sections, particularly Conservative and Catholic, in this country. If, after, it should appear that the forces of this particular Franco were made up very largely of Germans, who had come into the country as merchants, teachers, tourists, seamen

111

. . . would the behavior of the American Conservatives and American Catholics differ very greatly from that of British Conservatives and Catholics in similar circumstances in Spain?

8

American attempts to prevent Hitler accomplishing in Latin America what he has already accomplished in Spain would encounter a domestic obstacle, one rooted in American politics, much greater than any which faced Britain and France in the Spanish affair.

When British Conservatives not only failed to oppose, but by "nonintervention" most prodigiously aided, the German design to bring Spain within Nazi power, they did not have a justification which would most certainly have to be taken into account if America, after the defeat of Britain, attempted to oppose a similar German maneuver in Spanish America. There were not a million German-Britons and another million Italian-Britons and half a million Spanish-Britons forming part of the population of the British Isles during those years of appeasement. But the three or four millions of German speech and association, three or four million Italian and half a million to a million Mexicans of the South East are potential Trojan horses which might make it extremely difficult for an American government to risk foreign war (for a war fought, say, in the jungles of Brazil is still a foreign war even though on behalf of the Monroe Doctrine) for the purpose of checking the growth of Axis power. The danger would still be far from United States soil—if not as distant as Manchuria from Britain, then as far as Abyssinia from Britain, or at least as far as Spain or Czechoslovakia. A United States government, not altogether oblivious perhaps of the importance of the German vote plus the Italian vote plus the Irish vote,[5] would turn a blind eye to the breaches of the Monroe Doctrine, involved in the presence

[5] It may be noted in this connection that while the American politician has often in the past had to wrestle with the complications of a German vote, an Italian vote, a negro vote, an Irish vote, a Jewish vote, he has never had to face an English vote. Is this because the English element is quantitatively unimportant? We know that not to be true. It is more considerable than any other single element, if not more considerable than all the other elements combined. But when the English come to America, the society to which they come is culturally, linguistically so akin to their own, that they are almost immediately absorbed. So that it is perfectly safe for a politician in his Fourth of July orations to twist the lion's tail and bastinado George III to his heart's content. There will be no retaliation from an "English vote."

of what were in fact German armies on the soil of this hemisphere. Someone in Washington indeed might propose the appointment of a non-intervention committee along the lines of the strange London institution of that name, of which more in a moment.

9

In any case that doctrine might be quietly dropped on behalf of peace, as other American doctrines, older than the Monroe Doctrine, such as the Freedom of the Seas, the Rights of Neutrals, have been dropped. To the American of thirty or forty years ago, it would have seemed absolutely inconceivable that this country should try to solve the problem of neutral rights, the right of American ships to an open sea, defense of American lives at sea—by simply abandoning all claims to those rights and withdrawing her ships. In that respect America has solved the problem of defense by not defending; thus, also in this respect, following the example of Britain during the years of appeasement; like Britain, retreating from positions which had been held tenaciously for generations.

But, again, if British and French experience is any guide, this retreat would not be indefinite: Britain retreated in Manchuria, retreated in China proper, retreated on the Austrian matter, in Abyssinia, on the Rhineland question, retreated at Munich, in Czechoslovakia. But suddenly, even Mr. Chamberlain and Sir John Simon saw that retreat could not be indefinite, or any defense, even of the country itself, would soon become impossible. On a certain Wednesday evening in the House of Commons Sir John Simon was still talking entirely on the old lines; was still declaring complacently that the Munich policy had been entirely successful; that it had kept Britain out of war; that it had saved civilization; that these suggestions for mixing in the quarrels of continental Europe were fundamentally wrong; that they deprived you of the control of your own foreign policy since it passed from your own country to that of a "lot of foreign nations" (his actual phrase). Forty-eight hours later, at Birmingham, Mr. Chamberlain was announcing the end of the old policy of nonintervention, and forecasting a guarantee to Poland, a guarantee to be given before relations with Russia had been settled, a fact of course, which presented Russia (and Germany) with all the best cards. The policy which would have been relatively safe, with every prospect of success if adopted seven or eight years earlier, before the rearming of Germany, before the arrival of Hitler, before the successful aggression of Italy, before the reoccupation of the Rhineland, and would have saved the world from war and defended Britain, was adopted when it had become a course of deadly peril. But it was adopted then because retreat of that kind must always reach a point where the choice is between a stand or complete surrender. When that point comes free peoples make a stand even if it is too late to be effective. Wisdom demands that the stand should be made before that point is reached.

So far America has followed the general line followed by Britain, the line, that is, of insisting in the early stages of the episode upon complete neutrality in the presence of aggression however gross; the public putting forward insistent demands for keeping out, for nonintervention, securing that position if necessary by a series of retreats, the surrender of rights long held. But we see, just as we saw in England, the feeling *against* that position steadily and inexorably rising—the explanation being, of course, the gradual emergence, through all the misty confusions, of the moral sense which must exist somewhere in us, or we could never have built a human society at all. First, the moral neutrality goes, any pretense, that is, that we are not taking sides; this is followed by some material aid to one side and some denial to the other. Britain adopted that course, with hesitations and incompleteness, and with the hope that somehow the victim of aggression would extricate himself in the Chinese case. Optimists said, "China has never been conquered" —and continued to supply Japan with materials of war. We hoped Mussolini would get bogged down in Abyssinia. "Wait until the heavy rains come." Franco, we said, would never tolerate German interference in Spain. When he had won, the Spanish people would soon rise and hoof out the Germans as they rose against Napoleon. "Give Hitler rope enough and he will hang himself."

There came the moment when all the wishful thinking and the illusions fell away and the British people saw the stark truth. It is impossible, of course, to say at what precise point America will see it so completely as to realize that this common danger of brute violence must be disposed of before any cause or purpose of a free people, any plan of economic and social betterment, can be pursued in any safety, can be secure from the danger of utter destruction, sudden and complete burial, like that which has overtaken the splendid plans of the Norwegians and the Finns and Danes.

Perhaps the full realization will only come after the collapse of the British fortress; and then, of course, America's task will be more difficult than ever. If action is thus halting, American experience, too, will follow British: the decision to do the right thing was taken by Britain just when the right thing had become more difficult to do than it would have been at almost any time in the preceding decade.

But the moment of resistance will come in America as it came to Britain; for the United States will decide, after all, to stand by the Monroe Doctrine, as Chamberlain decided after all to stand by the principles his previous policy had undermined.

10

It would then be discovered, of course, that the magnificent airports which had been established in Latin America for the purpose of commercial aviation with the New Europe and Africa (which Germany now ruled) were in reality German airports; that the deepened and enlarged harbors, the oil depots . . . were just German harbors, German oil depots. And suddenly from them— with no more negotiations than Holland or Norway knew, with no more warning than Rotterdam got—bombs would be falling upon American cities, skyscrapers and all; and American munition plants and railway bridges, reservoirs and gasoline stores, would be in flames, or blown up with mysterious rapidity, while the armies from Europe moved across into Mexico or Central America to the appropriately prepared bridgeheads, in the shape of harbors duly prepared for their reception—across a sea now completely commanded by the navies which were once those of France, and Britain and Holland, and Spain, and Greece, and Turkey, added to those of Germany, Italy and Japan.

At this point America would find that to no
country in the world could the Hitlerian strategy
"to destroy the enemy from within, to conquer
him through himself" be applied in some respects
so easily and so profitably as to America. For of
the countries he had rendered almost impotent
before he attacked them by internal division, none
had possessed so potent and powerful a potential
fifth column as this. You can't intern three million
Germans, three million Italians, half a million
Mexicans and some tens, perhaps hundreds of
thousand Irish. For one thing most of them
would, in the early stages of the conflict, be sincerely pro-American, patriotic and anti-Nazi.
But (again following the example of Britain) so
deeply rooted, so innate is the prevailing notion
that all wars are struggles between national
groups—between "the French" on the one side
and "the Germans" on the other—that almost certainly this country would do what Britain did at
the outbreak of war, regard all Germans, all
Italians not born here as potential enemies; and
all citizens who were (including the professional

Irish-Americans) as friends. So much would the immigrant German and Italian, for the most part desiring nothing more ardently than the defeat of the dictators from whom he had fled, be subjected to suspicion, discrimination, to the rising hatreds of neighbors, to arrests on trivial charges, to false charges of espionage, that they would all tend to be driven into one vast army of embittered and brokenhearted enemies of American "freedom." Britain's fatal refugee policy (which in some measure produced that kind of outcome) was followed as the result of emotions which those subject to them were passionately convinced were emotions of patriotism, of love of their fatherland, a determination to tolerate none of its enemies. In Britain the matter was not so serious as it would be here; the German and Austrian refugees subject to internment numbered hardly more than fifty thousand persons. But here foreign-born "enemy aliens" or the children of such, would run into millions.

And here also the problem would have a seriousness in other than the numerical aspect which it does not have in England. There might be revealed as existing in this country the elements of civil war to a degree not previously suspected.

More and more of recent years America has been dividing into two broad groups or classes: the newcomers and the old original Anglo-Saxon element. It is, of course, a commonplace observation, but we should note its importance in this context. These two distinct groups don't even speak the same language, for the English of the newcomers is hardly recognizable as the tongue spoken at Harvard and Yale and the other great universities and in the pulpits of the Episcopal and other Protestant churches. And these differences are usually accentuated by economic and social differences. The old order, established here for generations, have accumulated wealth and have come to occupy a social position to which the Wops and Heinies simply cannot aspire. Social vanities and resentments are quite often far more potent as motives than the motives which are supposed to actuate the "economic man." And the older order, the Anglo-Saxon element, is associated in the minds of the newcomers with the "British cause." The cause of Britain is in their view the cause of snobs, of the upper classes, the

Anglomaniacs, the wealthy, the exploiters. It is these, the legend runs, who got us into the last war, and are trying to get us into this. It becomes, in this respect at least for millions of Americans, a class war.

You have in this situation a complex of hostilities and cleavages which the expert psychologists of the Hitlerian world authority will know how to exploit advantageously; as indeed he is exploiting them already.

This problem in its acute phase—the phase in which the country found itself at war with great masses of the population desiring the success of the enemy—could have been avoided if while yet nonbelligerent the material resources of the country could have been mobilized with an effort as complete and thorough as though there were "actual" war. But until stimulated by "actual" war, a country seldom makes that kind of effort; its will is obscured by crosscurrents of old prepossession and pugnacities. First things are not put first.

———— ❦ ————

One or two considerations should be added to the foregoing.

It will be said: "All this is extremely speculative."

All planning ahead involves speculation. We shall run into events entirely unprepared, unless we ask ourselves: What kind of situation is likely to arise? What forces, what difficulties and obstacles shall we have to meet in it? It is precisely the disparagement of "speculation" which accounts for the fact that events have found the Allies all along unprepared. It is Hitler's German gift for "speculation" which has enabled him to be thoroughly prepared for situations as and when they arise; so prepared as to be able to overcome powerful but confused and unprepared enemies.

Chapter V

WHY SHOULD GERMANY
WANT TO COME?

What motive would prompt a country already gorged
with vast conquests, still undigested, to enter upon the
extremely hazardous task of attacking the United States?
A statement from Hitler himself.

It is often asked:

Why should Hitler want to come to the United
States at all? With unrest in his rear what motive
would impel so hazardous a venture?

That question, like so many similar ones, has
been answered by actual events. The Axis has
already taken action against the United States.
It has in effect said: Stop aiding Britain and
China, or fight. The power of the United States—
its economic and industrial power, the supply of
ships and airplanes—is already embarrassing
Hitler. Already it is clear that if he could easily

"eliminate" the United States, he would do so.
This country is already very much in his way.
It may get very much more in his way in the
future, even if he does defeat Britain; and he
will, if the opportunity presents itself, quite certainly "eliminate" the United States.

Let us examine a little more closely why the
desire so to do springs from the very nature of
the Hitlerian system.

Hitler, as we know, is haunted by the fear that
Germany, by a sudden combination of power
against her, may once again face the fate she
faced in 1914-18, when in the course of a year or
two a dozen states—including two great powers
now Germany's allies—lined up against her.
Once, to a friend of this writer's Hitler, after an
impassioned recitation of all that Germany went
through in the years following the last peace, put
a case in some such terms as these:

> If your country had gone through such ex-
> perience as ours would you ever again permit it
> to be at the mercy of its neighbors, ever allow
> it to be weaker than any possible combination
> that could be brought against it? It is a simple
> question, yes or no?
>
> If you are honest and have those normal feel-

126

ings of patriotism which are part of the nature of every healthy man, then you will answer that if your country had gone through that experience, you would rather die—you would give your life a hundred times to see that never again should your country be at the mercy of others.

Therefore I put it to you, without acrimony or animosity, that my very first duty as the leader of Germany is to see that by no possible chance can Germany ever again be at your mercy, because she would not merely be at your mercy, she would be at the mercy of the Allies whom I trust even less than I trust America or the British Empire.

Yes, I don't disguise my thought. As the only alternative to Germany being at your mercy, which I am determined she shall never be again, you must be at ours.

But then I have never disguised the fact that that is the alternative before great states—it is the challenge of fate which nature throws down to us, to all men. If you cannot take up that challenge, if you cannot back your faith with your lives, as we are prepared to do, then it is proof that your faith is worth less than ours.

But note what this means—this struggle to dominate others as the only alternative to being dominated by them.

Hitler invades Poland. Stalin argues: "If he

takes the whole of Poland, he will have such strategic and material advantage, that I shall be at his mercy. I must have compensation." Stalin takes not only half Poland but part of Finland, all of Latvia, Estonia, Lithuania. Hitler says: "He may dominate the Baltic. I must seize Norway, Denmark as a counterbalance." Stalin replies with the seizure of Bessarabia, which Hitler feels must be counterbalanced by the occupation of the whole of Roumania. And so on.

But power, like peace, is indivisible. If Japan triumphs in China, Stalin must, in order to meet that growth of power on the part of a rival, find counterbalance somewhere else, perhaps in China itself, sharing the Chinese spoils.

But the power of Russia is not all that Hitler has to fear in his struggle for the "domination of others as the alternative to the risk of being dominated by them." The continued power and prosperity of a great democratic state like America is a continued menace. Its very existence proves to his own people that his doctrine about the decadence and weakness of democracy is false. It gives to democrats the world over the permanent hope of liberation. It may form the nucleus of opposition to him on the part of those whom he has subjugated. Italy is already restive in the Nazi combination. Her economic position is extremely bad. "If America," may argue Hitler, "remains a powerful and successful democracy, with Italy and other European states drawing funds from their compatriots there, she may well become a serious center of disturbance. Then there is Spain and the relationship between anti-Fascist forces there and revolutionary elements in South America. The United States, so long as her position in the Western Hemisphere is preponderant, not only closes the New World to me, it opens it to subversive forces that may threaten me. With the center of the British Empire moved to Canada, the reasons for eliminating America, if I can, become stronger still."

In Hitler's interview the report of part of which was given on a previous page, he made these points:

> Note what being in a position never again to be at the mercy of our neighbors means. First, we must prevent coalitions against us. Second, we must prevent internal division, the growth of nationally disruptive forces on German soil.

Third, since the main factor which entered into our defeat was the blockade, we must have such control over all contiguous European territory that their resources shall be available for us in the event of war, ensuring a self-sufficiency great enough to off-set the blockade.

But of all the factors which defeated us the most important of all was internal disruption, break up. This is the most important, because once things begin to crack at the center, everything goes. We must have complete national unity. The discipline may at times have to be severe. But discipline is in our tradition, in our blood; and we shall not fail.

In that interview, by the way, Hitler justified outright his procedure of profiting for the purposes of bloodless victories by the weakness of others. My friend in describing that interview—which took place, of course, before the war—tried to give me the tone and attitude of the Fuehrer's speech (it was nothing less) and described it as running like this:

Look back for a moment at what has been accomplished in the five short years of Nazi power. There have been restored to the Fatherland lands and people which under the old politics could not have been restored short of vast wars. They have not cost the life of one German soldier. I knew how to profit by the weakness of others. Do you suggest—seriously, do you suggest—that as trustee of my nation I should have allowed those opportunities presented by the weakness of others to slip by? Had I done so there is no punishment that the old German gods could have visited upon me that would have been adequate to my unspeakable crime.

The weakness of others presents to nations of strength not merely an opportunity: it presents a duty. I believe that in the past your people would have felt that too. The weakness, vacillation, indiscipline of Germany's potential enemies, the proof that they are incapable shows to every clear-headed German where his duty lies.

We here in Germany are in the midst of chaos. We believe ourselves to be an island of order in a sea of barbarism, or semi-barbarism to the east and southeast. In the end it means we must either dominate that barbarism or share it. We intend to dominate it. There is no other way in which great societies have ever been able to build up and maintain their structures. That was your way in the days of your greatness. The idea that the strong should yield to the weak, that weak and strong should by some lawyer's device be put on the same plane in the world, is to give the world over to the degenerate, to betray the best in man in favor of the inferior. It is a moral perversion against which the strong and mighty revolt. Once you felt that way, too, when your power swept over all those lesser tribes. But now you hover and hesitate. You dislike to take sides. You feel, many of your people, that this Russian mass is in truth a menace to Nordic civilization, but you won't join us to fight it. So with your League. You ask us into it. But you will not fight for that either. You will not make it a reality. Yet you ask us to believe that it can defend us.

So we may have to determine this thing in the old way. It will be the test which from all time the gods have imposed. We face that great truth. We believe that it is the only way in which the best can rule the less good, to the ultimate benefit, we believe, also of the less good.

Chapter VI

WOULD A NAZI WORLD MATTER?

Some fear that this is a fight to "preserve the British Empire" as against a German Empire. To be trapped by that idea is to acquiesce in the creation of a slave world in which this civilization will be engulfed; to accept lamely a Dark Age which energy could avoid.

Some will doubt whether the mere acquisition of the political control of Europe (including the British Isles) will place in the hands of the Nazi authority the power to manipulate its economic resources for political ends in the ways indicated in a previous chapter. They will argue, as Colonel Lindbergh argues, that America can live and trade with a Nazi Europe and Asia dominated by Germany as easily as originally she lived and traded with a Europe and Asia dominated by Britain; that the change of flag means little.

Now it is perfectly true that in the Liberal

capitalist world of the nineteenth century, the economic importance of "flags" was small and that whether Germany or France held Alsace-Lorraine made little difference to the life of the outside world. Some of the most prosperous and advanced of all nations were little states, like Switzerland and the Scandinavian states, of small territory, proving that the lebensraum theory had on economic grounds little validity. I have sometimes challenged certain current theories by putting it to my countrymen that if the United States were to annex the whole of the British Empire there is not an ordinary Englishman who would lose a pound nor an ordinary American who would gain one as the result of the transfer.

But, however true such arguments, they are irrelevant to the problem raised for us all in the Nazi revolution. For the roots of that revolution, its motive forces, are not found in the desire for welfare of the great masses of the German people; its driving force is passion, the nonrational or subrational in men; the deliberate cultivation of the human tendency to "think with your blood," to prefer guns to butter because guns mean power over other men, power to dominate, to retaliate for real or imagined humiliations, "to lord it over the earth." It is a biased and twisted reading of history which would interpret it all in purely economic terms. Such reading would leave unexplained some of the greatest episodes in our human story: Mohammed with his military conquests as little as Jesus with his victories of another kind; as little the man who suffered death upon the rack as the Inquisitor who inflicted it; a Massacre of St. Bartholomew as little as a Father Damien.

To imply, as is so often done, that the change from a British Empire in Africa, India, Australia, New Zealand to a Nazi one would mean no more than the difference between the French Alsace of 1870 and the German Alsace of 1875 is simply to close our eyes to the facts of the world about us.

No one who has had the patience to read the preceding pages of this chapter will accuse the writer of any exaggerated respect for the susceptibilities of the British imperialists. But criticism blind to plain and obvious fact is worthless. And the outstanding fact of the British "Empire" this last fifty years is that there has gone on within it a process of de-imperialization so great that the Empire has in fact, as an empire, come to an end and has resolved itself into a world-wide association of states very loosely associated for defensive purposes. How far that de-imperialization has gone may be illustrated in the present position of the Irish Free State—a point upon which centers, strangely enough, some of the bitterest criticism directed at Great Britain in this country. Though still regarded as part of the Empire, the Irish Free State has, since the beginning of the war, been completely neutral—not a "neutral" in the American sense, but neutral in the sense that Brazil, say, has been neutral. The German Minister is still living in Dublin with a very large staff of "clerical assistants." Britain had until shortly before the war naval bases on the southern coast (just as the United States has now naval stations on British territory in Newfoundland and the West Indies). But out of respect for Irish susceptibilities Britain evacuated these bases just before the war, although they had been accorded to her under the terms of the Anglo-Irish Treaty. It was an entirely voluntary evacuation on Britain's part. It is suspected that members of the very large German Ministry in Dublin have access to these harbors and that they serve as bases of supply for German submarines. What is certain is that the task of protecting British ships from submarine attack is rendered immensely more difficult by the refusal of Ireland to agree to allow British forces to occupy these bases as provided for in that treaty. As Mr. Lees Smith (a member of the Labor government) stated the other day in the House of Commons, the loss of many a British ship has been directly due to British scruples concerning the neutrality of Ireland.[1]

This curious feature of Dominion status (every

[1] Mr. Lees Smith said:

"If Hitler did not beat them by invasion he would try to do so by blockade. They were already losing some 67,000 tons of merchant shipping a week. Most of the sinkings were presumably off the west coast of Ireland.

"If we could use the ports of Southern Ireland which we handed over a few days before the war, we could reduce these sinkings to a small figure.

"The world should realise what we pay for our principles. Scores of ships are being sunk and thousands of seamen drowned because we cannot even within our own Commonwealth, use ports for our Navy which without that Navy would share the fate of Holland and Denmark."

An interesting footnote to the statement of Mr. Lees Smith is that a few days before it was made, there took place in Chicago a demonstration against further aid to Britain in which were displayed banners carrying these words: "Britain rules the slaves in Ireland" and other banners with the advice: "Let Britain give freedom to Ireland."

Dominion has the right of neutrality in the case of war by the sister Dominion of Great Britain) is worth attention because it is a fact—really characteristic of the British Empire—still quite inadequately realized. (It is not generally realized perhaps that "oppressed India" is so far fiscally independent that for over twenty years she has made her *own tariff*, has used the right to put heavy duties upon British goods and foster by bounties a native iron and steel industry to the disadvantage of Great Britain. Nor perhaps is it realized that there are fewer British officials— civil servants—in the whole of the Indian continent with its three hundred and fifty million people than there are American civil servants in the single Borough of Manhattan.)

The Germans have regarded this kind of thing merely as evidence of indolent incompetence, or of the moral degeneration of a once dominant race become, by too easy success, soft and corrupt. It is not thus that they would impose their rule over a quarter of the earth, over the three hundred and fifty millions of India, or over the dark millions of Africa. They have made no secret of their racial theories; of their belief that there exists a special type of man, themselves, the Master Race, called by nature, by history, by biology, to govern and organize inferior and mongrel peoples, for the benefit of the superior. The theories have been applied already to the Poles, whose position as helots has become already the subject of very severe regulation. It is a punishable offense for German settlers in Poland using Polish laborers, now reduced in fact to the position of chattel slaves, to sit at table with the Poles or treat them as equals. The German organization of labor on a slave or semi-slave basis is gradually extending over a great part of German-dominated Europe. If that is the German attitude to Poles, what is it likely to be to the inhabitants of India, or of Africa?

And we can be sure that production on this new basis will be organized with amazing competence. The tanks which smashed their way through the French lines were in large part made in Czechoslovakia, a territory which Germany had only conquered a few months, in factories whose workers had looked forward to fighting Germany. German ammunition production has already been largely shifted to Poland to be out of the reach of R.A.F. bombers. Where sabotage becomes too troublesome in the factories, the Nazi administration does not boggle at wholesale shifts of population by the tens of thousands, of a scope never before attempted by governments.

The Germans have developed, as we know, a capacity for organization of a mechanical, dehumanized type, second to none. To use human beings in the mass as so much mere material, for vast operations, seems especially to appeal to the German mind—to the mind, that is, which has been produced by a long background of special culture and tradition. It accounts in part of course for their military success. But they tackle their economic, social, industrial and commercial problems, especially all problems of production, in just that way: by using, under centralized direction, vast masses of men as mere material, as robots, having no more voice in the purpose for which they are being used than if they were so much rubber or cotton. The harsh discipline, the mechanical co-ordination necessary for that kind of economic and social "engineering," has always in some degree come natural to Germans.

It is true, of course, that enormously powerful

"interests" would be tied to the maintenance—
and extension—of the Nazi power. The core of
that vested interest would be the members of the
Nazi party and those directly dependent upon
it and them; perhaps in all some fifteen or twenty
million Germans, making a closely knit corporation, a sort of glorified Tammany Hall, of cosmic
proportions, world wide in its sphere of operations; the inner circle forming a kind of pagan
society of Jesus; self-perpetuating, training its
neophytes from infancy, and attaching them to
the central order by offering them the one thing
which of all other things in the world most tempts
men, not merely for what it brings materially
(which is very great) but also for itself as an
intoxicant. That thing, of course, is power—
power over other men, quite commonly power
actually of life and death.

There is nothing new in this idea of a relatively small central order or party making itself
master of communities, many times greater than
itself. We have seen it applied successfully over
and over again in history: in varying forms it has
been the method of most great religions, of Mohammed, of the Christian Church itself during

much of the Middle Ages. It is the method of the Communist party in Russia.

Hitler has merely applied this method, first to the capture of the German people, and then through the instrumentality of the German state to the capture of a large part of the universe. Even if he did not intend to apply it to the whole universe, which the Nazi party are quite determined shall become its oyster, the preservation of what he has already would compel that course as the previous chapter has shown.

But because the suggestion that the difference between a German Empire and a British one is not a difference which need concern the rest of the world is precisely a very big feature indeed of German propaganda, and is effective, owing to prevailing ignorance of certain things which have been happening in the British Empire the last half century, some notes on that point seem indicated.

Chapter VII

WHAT IS THE BRITISH EMPIRE?

Most of the world is still ignorant of the fact that the British "Empire" has for the most part come to an end, been resolved into something which is certainly not an empire. Things which are not in the region of opinion or controversy but of accomplished statutory fact are largely unknown or ignored as if they had never taken place. A note on the British monarchy.

On the front page of the *Journal American* of Thursday, October 10, 1940, first column, under the heading "In the News" occurs this paragraph:

England never abandons anything—never any commercial benefit, never any military advantage, never any valuable territory, never any strategic harbor.

Can anybody possibly imagine England's abandoning more than 114,000 square miles of the richest lands in the Pacific?

Can anybody imagine England's giving up the great gold lands of the Rand?

Certainly not.

I would undertake with a little industry to find a hundred similar quotations from American newspapers, magazines, books of the last ten years.

Now as a matter of simple statutory fact, duly recorded in official documents, Britain gave up all "ownership" of the Rand Mines—all authority over the territory in which they are situated, all control of the government in whose territory they are now situated—some thirty years ago when the South African Union became a Dominion. The British Parliament and government can no more legislate for the mines of the Rand than they can for those of California or Siberia.

It has often been remarked that the most important news never seems to get into the newspapers. It is certainly news of some importance that over most of its area the British Empire came to an end as an empire many, many years ago; but no one seems to have heard of it.

The fact suggests questions about that "British propaganda" about which we hear so much. If there were really such a thing as British propaganda, it would surely have dealt with this myth, which Goebbels exploits so profitably that a great New York newspaper can thus state dogmatically as fact something which ceased to be a fact more than three decades ago. The truth is, of course, that the legend of a far-reaching, octopus-like British propaganda, has about as much validity as the Protocols of the Elders of Zion.

The strange political fabric we call the British Empire retains a name that has lost its former meaning. An empire is a political organization in which subject provinces or states are governed from an imperial center, an imperium. But we know that that does not describe the British "Empire." By far the larger part, and the most important part, is not governed from London at all. Canada is not governed in or from London, nor is Australia, nor New Zealand, nor South Africa, nor, in very important matters like tariffs, is India, nor the Irish Free State. The Dominions have become in fact independent states and the Empire, so far as they are concerned, a very loose alliance of those states, an association of independent democracies. The tendencies or forces which have produced this result and have abolished imperialism over so large a part of the earth's surface, which have enabled an Empire to transform itself into a Commonwealth—those forces have not suddenly stopped. They are still at work. India, which now possesses fiscal independence, the right to make her own tariff, is on the road to dominion status. When India has become in fact a Dominion, she will not be the last Dominion. The process goes on.

Almost daily German propaganda suggests that it is an obvious and gross injustice for a people of 45,000,000 to own a quarter of the earth, while others lack living space; that this involves an inequitable and iniquitous division of the world's resources. Into the minds of the neutrals is put an idea and a picture: the idea of the Empire as an estate owned by inhabitants of the British Isles for their sole profit and enrichment; and a picture of John Bull as an obese, plutocratic landowner, possessing more territory than he can use.

Of that idea or picture we can say:

First, that it is utterly false; a mystification only made possible by popular confusion, the misuse and misunderstanding of certain terms.

Second, that most of the neutral world accepts this false picture as a broadly true one.

Third, that large and powerful sections of opinion in Great Britain accept it as true.

Fourth, that eminent British officials, to whose care has been committed the presentation of Britain's case to the world, declare it to be true.

Fifth (as a consequence of fourth), virtually nothing whatever is done by British propaganda (which most Britons deem unnecessary), to correct a falsehood of great advantage to the German cause and disadvantage to Britain's.

Let us examine these statements.

The Empire is not an "estate" at all and is not owned by the people of Great Britain. Goebbels' picture is a complete illusion. Let any Briton reading these lines think how much of the Empire *he* owns: how much Canadian or Australian or South African property—farm land or houses or mines or railway shares—he possesses by reason of the fact that something like the British flag flies at Ottawa, Canberra or Pretoria. The "British possessions overseas" are *not* possessed by the British people at all; but by the people who live there. Inaccurate and misleading terms have betrayed our thought, causing us to confuse "owning" and "governing."

So far as most, and by far the most important part, of the Empire is concerned, Britain does not even govern it. Because Englishmen—and the outside world—commonly refer to the dominions as "Britain's overseas possessions," they seem to believe that they really do possess them. There is a vague idea, even among a good many British people, that in some way they, the British, govern Canada and Australia and New Zealand and South Africa and Ireland; that the laws Britain makes in some way applies to them, or that they can only make laws which have Britain's sanction; that they are obliged to join in Britain's wars; that a declaration of war by Britain makes them belligerents, as much as it makes Yorkshire or Cornwall; that their parliaments have something like the limited authority of the London County Council.

All that is a complete mistake, and involves an entirely false picture of what the Empire has become.

The Dominions are independent states, their governments in no way subject to Britain's. She has no more power to alter the laws which the New Zealand Parliament, for instance, makes than she has to alter the laws made by the parliaments of Holland or Brazil. It has all been laid down definitely and clearly in the Statute of Westminster (of which not one foreigner in ten thousand has ever heard). That Statute declares that "no act passed after 1931 by the Parliament of the United Kingdom will be deemed to extend to a dominion," that Britain and the dominions are "autonomous communities," "equal in status, in no way subordinate one to another in any aspect of their domestic or internal affairs."

To get a true picture of Britain's relationship to, say, Australia, we should think of that country as a nation quite as independent, in fact, as Belgium or Norway was before Hitler came; having its own parliament, making its own laws by that parliament; its own army and its own navy, controlled by its own parliament; devising its own tariffs (dominion tariffs often hit British trade very severely); passing its own immigration laws (some of which rigidly exclude certain classes of British subjects); appointing its own officials, its own foreign representatives (both Canada and

Australia have ministers in Washington and other capitals); having, indeed, its own colonies and dependencies (Australia has several in the Pacific); having power to remain neutral, if its parliament so decides, when Britain is at war (Eire is at present neutral, and the South African Parliament only voted for participation in the war by a not very big majority); having power to maintain full diplomatic relations with Britain's enemy, if it chooses (Eire still maintains normal diplomatic relations with Germany, and the German Minister is at this moment living peacefully in Dublin); and having power to select its own Governor General, representing the Sovereign, as two Dominions have recently done.

But, you will say, the King? The King is accepted by, say, the South African Union not as King of Britain, but as King in the South African Union, as a symbol of close association with other British Dominions.

While we must think—if we want a true picture of the Commonwealth—of Australia, New Zealand, South Africa as independent states, we should add in our minds that they are independent states forming a loose alliance with each other; an alliance not on any well-defined terms but based on a gentleman's understanding that they will help each other if and when one of the group gets into difficulties.

I would not for a moment minimize the importance of that bond. It is vital. But it does not in the least qualify my statement that Britain does not "own" the Empire and governs only a relatively small and diminishing part of it.

There has gone on for three-quarters of a century a really amazing process of de-imperialization. Britain has done her best to unconquer her conquests; dis-annex her annexations; turn what originally was an empire into a group of sovereign and independent nations.

What is true of the Dominions will be true of India tomorrow. She has had her own tariff-making powers since 1919 and is in most spheres already self-governing. Her march toward dominion status would be still more rapid but for differences between the great mixture of states, peoples, religions, castes, which we call India and British fears of an aggressor's use thereof.

The process of de-imperialization still goes on. In Britain's sixty-odd "possessions," there are sixty different forms of government; some—the most important—independent; somewhere a measure of control is retained by Whitehall.

In one case—Newfoundland—a Dominion asked for the suspension of dominion status for a time in order to carry out urgent financial regeneration, since as a completely independent state the country had become bankrupt. It felt that financial salvation could best be undertaken with Whitehall's help.

The West Indies possess legislatures or legislative councils, and have been working toward practical self-government (the West Indies will one day probably make a dominion). But Whitehall still retains considerable control, which is why the British government has assumed responsibility for financial aid to Jamaica and other islands.

But the world simply does not *know* of the degree of de-imperialization already accomplished, or does not believe it to be a reality. The maps of the Empire published everywhere are still all of the same color, which creates the impression that Canada is governed just like Gibraltar or Malta.

ALONE *OR* ALLIED?

The ignorance about the Empire, both abroad and at home, passes belief. Once, lecturing in a German university, a professor of political science flatly denied that Britain did not make the immigration laws of Canada, and in effect told me I was a liar when I insisted that the British Parliament had no more statutory power over the legislatures of New Zealand or Australia than it has over the legislature of Peru.

It was in November, 1932, that a suggestion was made in the Senate that Britain should settle her debt to the United States by selling Canada thereto. "When a man has debts, and more land than he needs," it was explained, "he sells some of it." It was on October 18, 1935, that one of the most eminent of American journalists said in a public address that the British government would have just as grave responsibility as the totalitarian states for the next war, "for though Britain possessed more than she needs, she won't give any of it up to prevent war."

"If valueless," argued another American, "why not give up the Empire?" To which the answer is that Britain is giving it up, to people who live there. If she does not give it up to totalitarian

states, it is because they would close these territories against her, and would use their resources
to subject her to their domination. Her hesitations in India about going too quickly toward
independence are rooted largely in such mis-
giving.

It is true that Britain has a profitable trade
with the dominions and India. So she has with the
Argentine and Brazil and the United States. It
is true that Britain has made preferential arrangements with the dominions at Ottawa—extremely
mischievous arrangements, in which, incidentally,
Britain got much the worst of it. But they are
arrangements made between independent states,
and there is no reason on earth (except the falla-
cious notions in our heads) why we should not
have made the same kind of arrangement with
France or Denmark or Norway or Sweden. Indeed, it is precisely what she ought to have done.

Many British people share Goebbels' view that
this is a war to retain their "imperial possessions,"
and to enable them "to continue their imperialist
and capitalist exploitation of subject peoples."
Those phrases may be found repeatedly in the
anti-war resolutions of British Left-wing organi-

zations, including Left-wing organizations in the universities. And the underlying economic assumptions about the British imperial position are not confined to the extreme Left.

On the extreme Right, the conservative-imperialist view is that if Goebbels' picture of Britain drawing great profits from its imperial position is not a true one, then it ought to be, and that we should make it true by crusading for a ring fence round the Empire, keeping it to ourselves, and keeping the rest of the world out. They repudiate the idea that we should extend the commonwealth by bringing into that kind of association all free peoples; giving, for instance, to Norway or Denmark the same economic rights and the same right to mutual protection which we give the dominions, pooling our power to maintain the law against aggression, violence, war.

Why did the British Empire cease to be an empire properly speaking, and resolve itself, in large part, into a loose alliance of practically independent states? Why did the mother country surrender the economic privileges of an imperial position in according fiscal autonomy to its daughter states? No other empire in the past has done this. Spain did not, nor Portugal, nor Holland.

The evolution, alike on its political and economic sides, has exceedingly interesting and significant aspects. If we cut beneath words and symbols to the underlying reality we see that there has taken place, what we have been assured again and again never could take place—changes of frontier, the creation that is of new frontiers, without war. Communities, originally part of an empire, have achieved separate political status in no way subordinate to that of the states of which originally they were part. That is to say, frontiers have been changed. There are states, independencies and sovereignties where originally none existed; and this thing has been produced without war. The independence for which the Thirteen Colonies had to fight is accorded to Canada even without bitterness. Territory is freely "given up."

But why did Britain so readily acquiesce, so readily surrender her power, more especially power over the fiscal policies of the component territories of the Empire? For what we have seen going on is a process of economic "de-imperialization," the surrender of economic control in the territories she has conquered. What explains this "de-imperialization"?

While we have had from writers of "Left" tendencies, both Marxist and anti-Marxist, a vast literature embodying the economic interpretation of imperialism, no one seems to have dealt with the economic interpretation of the abandonment of imperialism which has been by far the more considerable process. Why does not some "economic determinist" present us with an economic interpretation of the abandonment of Empire, of "de-imperialization"?

Much attention has been directed to exposing the capitalist roots of imperialism. Very little attempt seems to have been made to explain, in terms of economic motive, the capitalist retirement from imperialism, the process by which vast territories like Australia, New Zealand, Canada, the Cape, the Philippine Islands have passed out of the control of the imperial powers which originally conquered them, have ceased to be in matters of economic imperial territory, and have become or are about to become economically in-

dependent states. Arrangements like those made
at Ottawa are not in the nature of privileges imposed upon reluctant subject-provinces by an imperial center in London for the benefit of the
mother country, in the manner of the sixteenth-
century Spanish Empire, but are bargains made
between equally sovereign nations, in which the
Dominion of Great Britain does not necessarily
come off best.

The economic importance of the area which,
during the last sixty or seventy years, has become
de-imperialized, "unconquered," is infinitely
greater than that of the area of fresh conquests.
Yet while the economically less important has
been the subject of a vast amount of attention of
the kind described, the more important has been
all but completely ignored. It would be possible
to mention a score of American books in which
it is taken for granted that the annexation of the
Philippines was due to the pressure of capitalist
interest. Not one of those authors explains how
this thesis of capitalist pressure compelling an
imperialist policy is to be reconciled with the
quiet granting at a later date of complete independence to the islands. Similarly, many writers

have explained the Boer War as dictated by London financiers; they have failed to explain why, if the financiers desired and were able to dictate the Boer War and the conquest of Boer territory, they did not desire or were unable to prevent, the granting of a degree of independence to Boer territory which rendered impossible further dictation from London. The granting of tariff-making rights to the Indian Legislature raises similar questions concerning the real relationship of capitalist interests to conquest and its maintenance.

It is worth while perhaps to add a note as to the part which the institution of monarchy has played in the transformation of empire into commonwealth.[1]

The Crown does seem to have served a real purpose in providing the nations of the Commonwealth—the democracies of Canada, Australia, New Zealand—with a symbol, a pledge, which has enabled them to do what it has been so extremely difficult for states to do in the past: to combine all but complete independence of political units with a capacity for common action

[1] This relationship of the monarchy to the empire has been dealt with in the author's *Defence of the Empire,* and passages in that book are here paraphrased.

between those units when it is really vital. The British Commonwealth, made up of states too obstinately independent to accept any written and rigid Federal Constitution, has nevertheless managed to federalize the function which it is most essential of all to federalize, that of defense. With no written constitution at all, by means of just a "gentlemen's understanding" the world knows, for instance, that if Japan should invade Australia, the Commonwealth as a whole would stand for the defense of that particular member. The British navy is an instrument of Australian defense, although Australia pays not one penny piece to its upkeep. Australian resources, human and material, would be available for the defense of Britain and the Commonwealth as a whole although there is no article of any constitution which imposes the obligation.

In the development of such a relationship the monarchy has certainly played a part. But note in what way.

There has been within the Empire for two hundred years or more the same conflict which marks the development of society everywhere: the conflict between liberty and authority, between those who want freedom, independence, self-government and those who hold the reins of power, who sit in the seats of the mighty. In inducing the latter to surrender their privileges, in inducing Britain to agree to surrender bit by bit her rights over the colonies, the monarchy has proved extremely useful. In this sense: the fact that the colony, or dominion, was ready to accept the King as symbol of the common authority has induced the British Tory to make concessions which he would certainly never have made if that gesture of loyalty had been refused.

The preservation of the monarchy, like the preservation of other feudal forms and symbols, has provided a means of "face-saving" for those who, possessing privilege, are asked to surrender it. By allowing the incumbents of privilege to retain the symbol, the shadow, if you will, it has been immensely more easy to induce them peacefully to surrender the substance than it would have been otherwise. It sounds a little ridiculous to say that men will more readily surrender the reality of privilege than the name, the title, the station, but it is only ridiculous to those who have never really examined the nature of the human motive. Men ornamented themselves from vanity, long ages before they clothed themselves for comfort, if indeed comfort can be said to be the first consideration in most clothing, even today. Men will make sacrifices for the sake of "face," "honor," "respectability," that they would never make for purely material considerations. It is not psychologically possible for a man really to give up his life for an economic motive—unless he is more certain of those heavenly mansions than, in fact, most men are. But men in all ages and all countries have readily given their lives from other motives. A man will not commit suicide for profit (how can he?), but he will commit suicide to escape disgrace, dishonor, deprivation of respect, social ostracism. "It is vanity which makes the world go round." Rather should we say that it is the desire for respect, the deference, of others. When the motive becomes fierce and savage, it develops into a desire to humiliate others, to assert our superiority. Those who cannot see this and admit it as an almost universal factor of conduct that has to be taken into account, have not begun to understand the nature of the forces which explain human society. It is not a minor and secondary factor of the human conduct, but lies at the very foundation of things. Any contest, as Galsworthy shows in *The Skin Game*, will tend to degenerate into a desire on the part of each side to secure the humiliation, the admission of defeat of the other, unless there enters a certain tradition, a feeling on the part of each that he must do what he can consonant with the substance of his own claim, to save the face of the other.

This face-saving for the other side the British democracy has always been ready to accord the privileged classes by allowing them to keep the form and symbol of privilege—so long as the substance is, in fact, surrendered. Thus, in the steady pruning of royal and feudal power, the popular forces in Britain have had the sense, the courtesy, to refrain, usually, from exacting, by surrender of symbols, formal admission of defeat by monarch or aristocracy. The monarch in Britain, like the aristocracy, has retained unchanged the names, the phrases, the symbols, which belong to a completely feudal order of society. It is because this concession has been made, that peaceful settlement between the rival factions has come about. In effect, the popular forces have said to King and Nobles, "Keep your titles, keep your form of privilege, so long as the reality of our rights is granted. You shall retain," in effect, the commoners have said to the King (in some cases to the feudal order), "the right to pronounce decisions, but you shall pronounce decisions only on the 'advice' of your ministers, who shall be our nominees." This has made possible a rapid concession on the part of privilege, which would certainly not have been possible if the people, the popular mass that is, had in effect said to privilege: "You shall abdicate, not merely in fact, but in form. Not even the shadows shall be left you." This has so often been the habit in France, this tendency to regard the doctrine, or rather the symmetrical, neat and tidy formulation of the doctrine, as the all-important thing.

We have seen this same form of concession to face-saving, made in the evolution of the Empire into a commonwealth of independent states. Had the dominions, who are in fact today republics, started with a demand for the right of formal, symbolical republicanism, those claims would have been fought by the conservative elements in Britain to the death. But so long as the monarchy seemed to retain its place, so long as Britain did not have to make as it were the sign of surrender, almost any concession could be made. In any case the fact is, that claims to independence on the part of colonies, which, in the eighteenth century, meant bitter war between the colonies and the mother country, were granted to Canada and Australia in the nineteenth century without any war at all, without bitterness, and in a form which has enabled the British Commonwealth to solve (so far) the age-old conflict between freedom and authority, to make reconciliation between the two which does not seem to have been made so effectively ever before. The forces of the Left in Britain have shown a similar wisdom in their own particular conflicts with Torydom.

Just after the last war, when all parties were more or less busy drawing up constitutions for the new order, a certain small political party in Britain had put at the head of its proposals: "Republican form of government." One English veteran of the Labor movement spoke thus:

> Put the word "Republic" at the head of your programme, and you will spend the next two generations fighting wastefully, hatefully, spilling blood, over shadows and symbols, and we

shall never get to questions of social welfare at all. You will spend your lives tilting at windmills. And possibly in the end windmills will defeat you. Make the concession of form on your side and you can get, with infinite greater ease, the concession of the substance from the other.

What, he went on to ask, did they want? Slum abolition, control of industry, old-age pensions, minimum wage, work or maintenance—did these things come first or last? If they wanted them to come first, "concede the King."

But while the retention of old symbols of sovereignty, archaic terms of feudalism, have been enormously useful in making the surrender of ancient privilege easier, of taking the edge off that surrender, of easing the transition from imperialism to internationalism within the confines of the British Commonwealth, the continued employment of those terms has made it difficult for foreigners—if not indeed for Englishmen themselves—to appreciate just what is taking place, or what has taken place, in the "Empire," to see realities beneath the names and the symbols. And it is important to see the realities.

Chapter VIII

WHY WERE THE BRITISH BLIND?

The trend of events which undermined the security of the empire has been evident for the last ten years and was foreseen by some even before the end of the last war. Why were British statesmanship and the British public blind to these dangers for so long? Some of the confusions and prejudices which explain the blindness.

A good many American books have been written this last year or two—like the admirable book of Mr. John F. Kennedy—to explain "Why England Slept," why she was oblivious to the dangers which have brought her particular world, the kind of world by which she lived in her free way to ruin; so much of it to irreparable ruin. Surely that outcome carries for Americans a certain pregnant suggestion.

Here were a people, who had managed in a few generations to build up the greatest—and the freest empire or commonwealth of states that history has ever seen. Their system was world wide. While they certainly did not "own" a quarter of the earth, they certainly influenced powerfully more than a quarter of its population. The achievement points to the possession of a practical political sagacity and judgment—a sagacity which Americans in the past have tended rather to over- than to underestimate. (The legend of an almost satanically competent foreign office for which there is alas! exceedingly little foundation, has been very common in the United States.)

But that overestimate surely prompts a question: If a people, politically as competent as these, committed mistakes on the scale which their disaster indicates, is it not just possible that Americans also, may be capable of similar mistakes—unless they profit by the experience, particularly by the errors, of others? Ought not this country to assume that if a people as politically wise as the British could fall into fatal and destructive traps they must be well hidden traps into which others can easily fall, unless extremely vigilant.

How can we detect those traps? What are the signs?

ALONE *OR* ALLIED?

Excellent as Mr. Kennedy's book is, its title is in some degree misleading. For to imply that Britain's disaster—or Europe's—was due to somnolence, is to distort the nature of the malady which has brought Britain so low. Her disaster has been due to the fact that very many of her people were active in the pursuit of mistaken ends; not sleepy, but passionate, hitting out blindly, but often with maniacal energy to destroy the very policy which might have saved them. Those who attempted to reveal the traps set for Britain's destruction, were often either treated with contumely and contempt (in the early stages of the slide to disaster as "Pacifists" and in the later stages as "warmongers") or attacked with passion and violence—the sort of violence which marks the deep sincerity of isolationists in America in their attacks upon the interventionists.

It is fashionable, in explaining the collapse of Europe before the Nazi advance to talk of "corruption" and "softness," of failure to provide a social order which the people could deem worth defending; or of failure to arm. But it is quite clear that many of the democracies which have perished were not corrupted or degenerate or possessed of social systems their people did not value, nor indisposed to arm.

Take Finland. She was not "soft," heaven knows, nor "corrupt," nor had she failed to create a social system her people valued. Nor was she lacking in valor. Nor did she lack a carefully prepared defensive system. For years she was regarded as a model state, and the dauntless courage and unity with which she faced the Russian invader moved the world. But in the end she was overcome. And she would have been, however much she had developed the qualities and values just enumerated. She might have spent ninety per cent of her total resources upon arms. And she would still have been at the mercy of Russia's brutal, dull preponderance of human flesh and weight of metal. Nothing could have saved Finland from the might of Russia, save combination with other states to create a common defense for all of them, based on the principle that an attack on one was an attack on all. And that policy neither Finland nor her neighbors followed with much energy, though they could have been induced to accept it had it been proved that the great powers—particularly Britain and France—really meant business in their talk of collective defense against aggression.

Take Norway. She, also, was in many respects a model state. Yet, whatever efforts she might have made, standing alone would have been futile in resistance to Germany. In her case too, it could be said that she had to make her defense collective or renounce it altogether. So with Denmark. So with Holland. So with Belgium.

Now is this true or not? It is undeniably true; it is self-evident.

No one of these states fighting by itself alone could possibly defend itself. Yet this undeniable and self-evident truth the Western democracies would not face, or would not face sufficiently to make it the basis of their defensive policy. Nor would they, nor did they, squarely accept the logical alternative of Pacifism. Nearly all of them made very considerable preparations for defense. Holland was under arms, spending what was in proportion to her total budget positively killing sums upon the maintenance of a state of mobilization for a year before she was invaded. Belgium had considerably over half a million men under arms when she was attacked. But though these states—like the great powers—would make all these military preparations for defending themselves, their own soil, they boggled egregiously and finally refused to commit themselves in any way to the defense of others, of each other. This principle, already indicated in a previous chapter, the principle "we will fight for ourselves but we have no interest in fighting for others and will not do it"—the slogans which had such immense popular appeals—made their downfall in the end inevitable. It was the popularity of nationalist isolationism, "let us have no truck with untrustworthy foreigners," which has placed the whole of Western continental Europe under the domination of Hitler.

The retort—and it is no more than a mere retort—to that suggestion is that Britain and France did have a collective system and that it broke down "proving it won't work."

Well, it is possible of course that the collective system cannot work; that men have not sufficient intelligence to maintain a system of co-operation between free peoples, to hang together as the only alternative to being hanged separately. In which case, it is the end of the matter and the end of free civilization; and time that we stopped concerning ourselves with defense against aggression at all. For resistance will be futile if those who propose to profit by violence and aggression prove that they *can* combine for their ends, while we who would resist prove that we cannot combine for ours.

As a matter of fact French and British collective action broke down precisely because the countries concerned rejected, at crucial moments and crucial points, the obvious truth that unless each unit of the collective system is prepared to fight for others, as well as himself, that system cannot exist at all. From the moment that it became a question of defending the combination, and not merely each his own country, its soil or its possessions, it was found that war was a wicked thing; not wicked when used to defend ourselves, wicked only when used to defend others, the combination or constitution under which others as well as ourselves might find defense.

It is the denial of this truth that we are members one of another which explains the failure of the democracies to meet the Nazi power.

AMERICA'S DILEMMA:

The supreme and fundamental danger in Western Europe has always been the denial of that truth.

Even before the end of the last war, this present writer was insisting that unless it was recognized, the victory over Germany could not possibly be permanent. In a book published in May, 1918,[1] he wrote thus:

> The survival of the Western democracies, in so far as that is a matter of the effective use of their force, depends upon their capacity to use it as a unit, during the War and after. That unity we have not attained, even for the purposes of the War, because we have refused to recognize its necessary conditions—a kind and degree of democratic internationalism to which current political ideas and feelings are hostile; an internationalism which is not necessary to the enemy but is to us.
>
> For the Grand Alliance of the Democracies is a heterogeneous collection of nations, not geographically contiguous, but scattered over the world; and not dominated by one preponderent State able to give unity of direction to the group. The enemy alliance, on the other hand, is composed of a group of States, geographically contiguous, dominated politically

[1] *The Political Conditions of Allied Success* (Putnam's).

174

and militarily by the material power and geographical position of one member who is able by that fact to impose unity of purpose and direction to the whole. If we are to use our power successfully against him in such circumstances, during the War, at the settlement, and afterwards (which may well be necessary), we must achieve a consolidation equally effective. But in our case that consolidation, not being possible by the material predominance of one member, must be achieved by a moral factor, the voluntary cooperation of equals—a democratic internationalism, necessarily based on a unity of moral aim. Because this has not been attained, even during the War, disintegration of our alliance has already set in—involving military cost—and threatens to become still more acute at the peace. The enemy group shows no equivalent disintegration.

No military decision against the unified enemy group can be permanent if at the peace table it becomes evident that the Western Democracies are to revert to the old lack of consolidation, instability of alliance, covert competition for isolated power and territory, and a national particularism which makes common action and co-ordination of power cumbrous, difficult, or impossible.

The factors of disintegration in the Grand Alliance include conflicts of economic interest and social aspiration within the nations, more dangerous with us than with the enemy, because our historical circumstances have rendered us less disciplined or less docile, less apt in mechanical and de-humanised obedience.

The general truth we are here dealing with is of far greater importance to us than to the enemy. He can in some measure ignore it. We cannot. His unity, in so far as it rests upon moral factors, can be based upon the old nationalist conceptions; our unity depends upon a revision of them, an enlargement into an internationalism. . . . Some "permanent association of the nations" by which the security of each shall be made to rest upon the strength of the whole, held together by the reciprocal obligation to defend one another.

And since that date of 1918—now more than twenty-two years ago—this writer has continued to insist that if arms are to defend us, those who are defending broadly the same thing, must pool their arms; must develop the factors of political co-operation by which alone the arms can become effective. He has related that truth at various times to the various disastrous stages of the appeasement policy in books all more or less telling the same story.

ALONE *OR* ALLIED?

One runs into the danger of complete mis-understanding and confusion at the outset by the very use of such words as "Collective Security," "League of Nations." For men take such phrases, make of them a label for a certain plan or scheme as they see it in their minds, decide such a plan is unworkable and then, dismiss as unworkable the principles which those plans tried to embody.

The League of Nations, as established at Geneva, may have been utter folly, should never perhaps have been started in that way (that happens to be my view). But underlying it was a principle of policy, that of common action by free peoples against aggressive war, war as an instrument of national policy. There are a hundred different ways in which that principle could be applied by a group of states. The way is secondary if the will to apply the principle to international relations at all be there. And that will in the last resort depends upon understanding.

The workability of any constitution depends upon the degree of understanding of its essential principle by those who have to work it. The British people have made a fair success of con-stitutional government. But they have no constitution; it does not exist as a cut and dried document. What gives them constitutional government is the understanding by parliament and people of one or two basic principles. One such principle is that if a political party, however good its platform, should attempt to enforce its claims by violence, war, all parties should at that moment combine to resist the attempt, and to support the constitution. It is recognized as an absolutely vital principle that the job of a great military commander is to enforce the constitution not dictate to it, however popular he or his cause.

Where this recognition of the right place of force in the state is not clear, as it has not always been among the people of certain Latin-American republics, it serves no purpose to give them the most perfect constitution in the world. It won't be worked. It is no good giving the nations, as they were given at Geneva, a pretty good constitution, if there is absent a general realization of "where force belongs."

The League was an attempt to express the constitutional principle. That principle is, after all, the foundation of organized society: the power of the community must protect the individual citizen against another's violence. If the community, the state, did not thus protect its members the members would not support it, and it would dissolve.

If, when within the nation an armed individual or powerful corporation under some sense of grievance, it may be, possessed himself, or itself, of the possessions of others, taking the law into its own hands and making itself judge in its own cause, we, as the community, then proclaimed our "neutrality," insisting that it was no affair of ours and that we were not going to intervene—if we took that attitude of not being concerned in the defense of others from violence, it would be the end of security for anyone. Within the nation we use our combined power in a certain way—to uphold the constitution and the law designed to protect those who (as by their taxes) contribute to its force. We see that if law or constitution is to exist it must protect those living under it. Otherwise they won't support it (why should they?) and it will have no power. We recognize as obviously true when we think of our national society that if we are not prepared to defend others—the constitution, or law, or rule, or code

which defends others—that it will be impossible
for our power to defend ourselves; that power
used individually can never ensure effective defense and security; that unless defense is collective there can be in the long run no defense for
anybody. All this we recognize when we think of
security within the nation; all this we deny when
we think of security as between nations. Again
and again the opportunity came—in the Manchurian business, in the Abyssinian affair, in
Spain, in the Rhineland—to assert that truth in
policy, and again and again the opportunity of
so asserting it and making it part of the British
policy, as Monroe made one aspect of that truth
part of American policy, was allowed to slip. The
principle was not so much challenged as disre-
garded. It was either smothered in other pre-
occupations or it became entangled with certain
prejudices, prejudices of the kind which men
would rather take the risks of death and muti-
lation than surrender.

And now, once more, fate gives the remaining
democracies one more chance to recognize that
truth, build their action upon it, and save the
relatively free and humane civilizations of the

American Union and the British Commonwealth from the fate which has overtaken the democracies of continental Europe.

The fault of the failure so far lies, in the view of the present writer, as these pages show, mainly with the governments of Britain which existed between 1931 and 1939. But if history is to record another failure, the guilt will not be entirely that of the government of Britain. For precisely those prejudices which have frustrated right policy so often on the part of Britain seem now to be operating in the United States, not, it is true entirely to frustrate policy because it moves in the right direction, but to delay it, render it at times hesitant, and inadequate.

In his introduction to Mr. Kennedy's book, Mr. Henry Luce writes that he regrets that "Mr. Kennedy has not devoted more attention to the practical possibilities of what was called collective security. The post war world," continues Mr. Luce, "had an idea. That idea was collective security." It was, he adds, the idea over which Hitler triumphed. Why did it fail? It failed in Britain for about the same reasons that it failed in the United States.

Mr. Kennedy refers, very justly, to the criminal negligence or folly of Sir John Simon in the matter of Manchuria. But the real criminal was less a man (great as his responsibility is) than a great public confusion. This idea to which Mr. Luce refers was, it is true, "accepted" by the public—most ardently, by the way, in America in the years 1916-1919 with the all-but-universal advocacy of a League to Enforce Peace (with accent on the enforce)—but not in truth understood. About it there prevailed certain confusions which ended by destroying it as a practical policy.

If Mr. Eden's resignation did little more than check for a moment the continued repudiation of the principles for which he, and Mr. Churchill, stood; and if Mr. Churchill had to wait until the Empire had been brought to appalling disaster before the House of Commons would so shake itself from the rut of party allegiance and the party machine as to replace a government rapidly bringing the country to ruin, it was because neither parliament nor the country appreciated *in time* the difference between the principles which Mr. Churchill (or even Mr. Eden) would have applied and which Mr. Chamberlain was applying. There were, it is true, elements in Great Britain who understood clearly that difference and would have put Mr. Churchill into power. But the part of the public which was able to determine policy still preferred to cling to the prejudices which stood in the way of the necessary change.

In Britain the prejudices were not difficult to discern. Most on the Right confused the whole idea of collective defense[2] with vague international schemes of world regeneration, "this League nonsense." In many quarters of the Left, collective security was dismissed as not going to the root of the thing because "the real cause of war is Capitalism; Capitalism is incompatible with Peace; get rid of Capitalism and you will get rid of war." (In this connection I used to point out that capitalism was not incompatible with peace as between, say, Maine and Massachusetts, or Pennsylvania and Ohio, but would probably have been if they had evolved, as did most of the Spanish colonies, to the status of completely independent nations; that what has made

[2] Mr. Churchill remarked at that time in his inimitable way "the only thing absurd about collective security is that it does not exist."

183

peace possible between the States of the Union, in contradistinction with the nations of Latin America is not something economic, the abolition of capitalism, but something political, the introduction of Federalism.)

One dominating confusion which bedeviled sound judgment was this: The League and collective security were accepted as the *alternative* to arms and force, and not as the means by which (and so far as their underlying principle is concerned, the only means by which) arms and force can be made effective for defense. Men seem to get a vision of two pictures: On the one side they see arms, battleships, airplanes, guns, cannon; things which they know are dreadful instruments of unimaginable horror. On the other side they see a vision of peace, conciliation, good will, institutions of law. It seemed to many that you had to choose one or the other. They refused to see that you could only get the latter by the proper, instead of the improper, use of the former.

It is true that in the period of the League to Enforce Peace, Americans were full of the right argument:

184

ALONE *OR* ALLIED?

The way to have peace, the way to see that the German tragedy is not repeated is for everyone to undertake to combine against the war maker, to jump on the criminal who would make war in order to enforce his own judgment in a quarrel with a neighbor. No litigant ought to be judge in his own cause. It is a denial of elementary right to the other litigant. Let us, therefore, arm the law—the one law that nobody shall go to war, the law to be upheld by everybody undertaking to oppose the nation that refuses arbitration.

What happened to it?

When it came to be embodied in a rudimentary constitution of free nations, it was discovered that it meant this country "taking sides in an European quarrel"; it meant, it was argued, making every local war a world war; it meant undertaking to go to war. (Obviously, since that was the whole basis of the plan. There could be no collective action to resist aggression without that undertaking.) But the discovery seemed to come as a dreadful shock to peace-loving Americans, the idea that after a great and destructive war, the world should start upon a system of peace by nations undertaking to go to war. And then, of

185

course, attention began to be diverted to issues much nearer at hand, issues of domestic politics, in which the more remote foreign problem became buried, or became an issue to be played with as part of the game of party politics, very much as Britain's gross error at the time of the Manchurian business was explained in part by the fact that the issue came before the British public just at the moment that the country was being pushed off the gold standard, was confronted by national bankruptcy and was in the throes of forming a "national" government.

There is usually indeed a certain lack of intellectual honesty in the statement of our desire for peace. Statesmen commonly declare that above all they desire peace. British statesmen for years have been saying: "The greatest interest of the British Empire is Peace." They have been sincere in saying it, but, of course, they did not believe it. For if British territory had been attacked they would have abandoned a condition of peace and produced a condition of war by resistance. That is to say, they preferred war to foreign domination. Their greatest interest therefore was not peace; their greatest interest was freedom from foreign domination, defense. They (rightly) put defense before peace.

This writer has, therefore, insisted: that if what you really want is defense, the problem is to discover how to combine defense with peace, which can only be done by the "constitutional" method, applied to the relations of such states as are prepared to use force "constitutionally," in resistance, that is, to violence attempted by one member of the group against another. By that means, and by that alone, if human experience goes for anything, can violence be exercised.

In September, 1938, the opponents of collective security asked how we could possibly aid in the defense of Czechoslovakia (the same question could as suitably be asked of our commitment to Poland). The place to have defended Czechoslovakia was eight years previously in China. Had we defended order then—by diplomatic and economic aid to China, leaving the war declaring to be done by Japan—Czechoslovakia would not have been destroyed.

If in 1939 it was wise to meet the menace of Fascist aggression by collective security, it would have been wiser still to have met that menace in some such way in 1931, in the case of Japan, and before Fascism had become world wide and had acquired terrifying power.

Consider for a moment.

In 1931 Hitler had not yet come to power; Germany was not yet rearmed; the Rhineland was unfortified; Italy was not established in Abyssinia; German guns were not mounted opposite Gibraltar—none of these threats existed. Mr. Stimson and President Hoover were anxious to secure British co-operation in refusing recognition of Japan's conquest of Manchuria, adding the Stimson doctrine of nonrecognition to the Monroe Doctrine as part of America's diplomatic armory. America had declared her willingness to co-operate with the League in any measure to restrain Japan. Russia was anxious to see Japan checked. If *then*, Britain had accepted cordially the American offer instead of coldly rejecting it; had furnished economic aid to China in her resistance to Japan instead of imposing an embargo which worked entirely to the advantage of Japan; had given China moral support instead of morally espousing the cause of Japan, had drawn closer to Russia; if, in other words, Britain had adopted eight years earlier the policy adopted much later, Japan's course of conquest would have been rendered so difficult that Mussolini would not have been tempted to follow in Abyssinia the Japanese example nor to have invaded Spain. We should have had neither the Abyssinian war, nor the Spanish invasion, nor the annexation of Austria, nor the conquest of Czechoslovakia.

The policy which Britain at last adopted toward an immensely strong Germany was, when suggested as the appropriate attitude to Japan, described as "making war as means of securing peace." There was, of course, no question of "making war on Japan," and the charge so commonly made that the policy involved such a course is due to strange confusions. If China had been helped, economically and diplomatically, by British, American and Russian co-operation, we should then have left it to Japan to do the war declaring, and stood on the defensive. It is unlikely that Japan would have declared war at one and the same time upon four hundred million Chinese, a hundred and sixty million Russians, the United States and the British Empire. There would have been no war, and instead of such action turning a local war into a world war, as was predicted at the time, it is precisely the failure to take that action which *has* turned a local war, which began in Manchuria, into a war in Abyssinia, in China proper, in Spain, in Poland, in France, in Britain.

The common assumption is that if a state is guaranteed security it will adamantly refuse to make any concessions on behalf of necessary changes in the *status quo*. But the contrary comes nearer to the truth. Suppose a state has within its borders a national minority and is asked to cede the minority area. To do so weakens the state strategically. It says to Europe: "If as the result of weakening myself, by making this concession, I am attacked, will you, my neighbor, Europe, help to defend me?" And if the neighbors, repudiating such commitments as dangerous, say "no," can we reasonably expect the state in question to make the concession? Security is usually the condition *sine qua non* of peaceful change. To weaken the guarantees against war with some muddled idea that, by allowing the strong now and again to have their little war of conquest while we look the other way, we may bring about the necessary changes with the least risk to ourselves, is precisely the type of imbecility which has brought us to our present pass.

To allow the strong to enforce territorial redistribution by war, prompted by the idea that redistribution so secured will make for peace, is to disregard all experience and the most elementary logic of the situation.

Not only do changes made at the will of the victor after war inevitably create as many problems as they solve, but they do not solve *the* problem of war, which is security, that self-preservation which is as much the first law of life with political as with other living organisms. Where self-preservation depends upon the preponderant power of the individual (whether state or person), upon being stronger than those who might attack us, there can, obviously, be no such thing as general defense, for the defense of the stronger in that case is purchased at the cost of sacrificing the defense of the weaker. Only when the law—primarily the supreme law that there shall be no war, that none shall be the victim of his neighbor's violence—is upheld by a sufficiently large group of the human community, can defense become generalized, reconcilable with justice.

If I demand the right to be stronger than my neighbor, I claim a right of defense by superior strength denied to him; if I propose to use my strength to be judge of disputes between us, I claim for myself a right of judgment denied to him.

By no possibility by that method can there be equality of right. If I ask him to submit, not to me or to my power, but to the law by which I myself am prepared to abide, there *is* equality of right.

We see here why the last Great War came, why victory was futile, why war came again.

We would not tolerate the preponderance of Germany, her threatened domination of the world—that is to say, of ourselves. We demanded, in effect, that *we* should have preponderance. When we got it we used it to make the Treaty of Versailles, sufficient proof to Germany that our preponderance was incompatible with justice to her. She now, once more, intends preponderance. Do we now once more propose instead to impose our own? But if we could not make our preponderance permanent before, why should we hope to do so "next time"?

If the relationship of great powers is always to be marked by that futile and dreadful oscillation, then truly will civilization, order, mercy, perish from the earth.

We must not, we cannot, ask Germany once more to accept our domination, to be used once more for another and a worse Versailles. We must ask her to accept the domination of the law which we ourselves are prepared to accept, the law that none shall use violence, war, in order to be his own judge in his own cause. She must submit, not to us, but to law; to which we submit.

But unless we are prepared to do as much for that law, to make for it sacrifices as great as for our own possessions, it can never have power to protect men.

This writer has always taken the view that the ordinary citizen, the voter, the plain man, is entirely capable of understanding social problems sufficiently to direct society to his purpose; that in order to insist upon wise foreign policies he does not need to have the specialist's knowledge

of obscure ethnographic problems of the Balkan
or Danubian areas, or their complicated politics,
or the precise degree of justice in the claims of
the Sudeten Germans. But he does need to have
a comprehension of certain broad social principles, an understanding which ought to be the
possession of every member of a democracy. The
ordinary man cannot know, and does not need to
know the merits of such disputes as that which
preceded the Japan-China, or the Italy-Abys-
sinia, or Germany-Czechoslovakia crises. What
he does need to know is that such disputes should
not be settled by the violence of the stronger party
imposing his partial judgment on the weaker and
that if such a method of eliminating the weak by
the strong is tolerated, his own turn to be eliminated will surely come. But the one point of
principle which is not only vital but quite within
the comprehension of the layman because it is
part of the familiar mechanism of all organized
society, is precisely the principle which becomes
obscured in great international crises by the discussion of details which the layman cannot decide
and does not need to decide.

In every one of the cases in which we in Britain

have refused aid to the victims of aggression and violence we have entered, sometimes quite violently, into the merits of the dispute. Were we quite sure that China was blameless? After all, Italy did need room for expansion. The Spanish government had been guilty of atrocities . . . and around such disputes controversy raged.

Now the whole purpose of that collective defense of law (which its critics declare to be "coercion") is the prevention of violence, prevention of the exercise of coercion by one of the parties to the dispute over the other. It was not for British Cabinet Ministers or British editors to decide the rights and wrongs of a dispute between Japan and China or Italy and Abyssinia or Germany and Czechoslovakia. It *was* our obligation, bound as we were by the Covenant, to do what we might to see that the dispute was not settled by the violence of one of the parties. Our function was the prevention of violence, not the settlement of disputes, which should have come before properly constituted bodies of conciliation or judgment as the case might be.

In newspapers of the weeks preceding the 1938 crisis you will find elaborate (and ignorant) dis-

cussion of the precise extent of the Sudeten grievances ("What is the seating capacity of the German as compared with the Czech school?" . . .
"Would not small Cantons" . . .) as though
that and not the right of the last remaining democracy east of the Rhine to independent existence free from Nazi domination, and the survival
in Europe of some corporate sense of law and
right, were the real issue; and as though the re-
dress of Sudeten grievances were the purpose of
German intervention; as though it were not the
very last thing that Hitler desired.

To be trapped into the elaborate discussion of
the details of that dispute instead of concentrating
upon the one task of preventing its settlement by
the violence of the stronger party was to render
its just or peaceful settlement impossible. Our
public were no more competent to judge upon
those details than the readers of picture papers
are competent to pass judgment in the latest mur-
der trial now *subjudice*.

It was quite a big enough task to do what we
could to fulfill our promise to defend the weaker
party against the violence of the stronger to the
end that the latter should not, by mere virtue of

its greater force, become judge of the cause—which is what has happened.

Note still further strange confusions. We had undertaken to build up a system the purpose of which from first to last was the prevention of violence and coercion, the leaving of the settlement of disputes to properly constituted authorities. It is objected to by very many on the ground that coercion is so bad a thing that we must not attempt to aid its victim, though that refusal of aid makes violence by one of the parties to a dispute tempting and easy. Further, because we should not interfere in the disputes of others, *we* will decide a complicated issue like that of the Sudeten Germans and conclude, by virtue of *our* decision, that the use of violence, or the threat of it, by one of the parties to the dispute is justified.

Because we did not see that the first purpose of power is to prevent war, not settle disputes, we failed to secure just settlement of the dispute and failed to prevent the growth of war. The real issue of September, 1938 was not the precise extent of the grievances of the Sudeten Germans (and the last thing we should have done was to have sent Runciman to pass upon a question

which has baffled experts of twenty years' standing) but whether one more bastion in the defense
of European law and freedom should fall;
whether the living body of a once free state
should be delivered over maimed and helpless to
the tender mercies of the Gestapo, to Goering, to
Goebbels and to Himmler.

Yet beneath the intellectual confusion there
was a moral failure. Let us see of what kind.

Chapter IX

ERROR AND ATONEMENT

> In the last analysis, the disaster which has come upon
> Britain is the recognition, too long delayed, of certain
> moral truths, a delayed awakening of a certain moral
> sense. But Britain is making her atonement nobly and
> in full.

What the story told in these pages amounts to
is this:

European society, developed along the lines of
freedom, that is to say, based upon the right of
men to decide what shall be done with their lives,
the right to have access to knowledge of the facts
relevant to that decision, the right to discuss the
facts among themselves so that their judgment of
the facts may be sound—such a society has been
unable to defend itself against the challenge of a
relatively tiny group of men, the inner circle of
Nazi and Fascist parties. This relatively small

group challenge that right and say in effect to the majority: You shall live, not as you may desire, but as we shall determine; your lives are not yours but ours, to do with as we will.

Society has been unable to meet that challenge of a relatively small number of violent, cruel and merciless men because owing to confusion concerning what may be called the mechanism of its defense, it has repudiated the principle by which alone a majority can defend itself against a criminal minority. That principle is an extremely simple one. It is this: If the majority is to defend itself against crime, it must stand together as a unit, a corporate body. For if the majority will only, in defense, act as individuals while the criminals in their aggression combine together, then the majority is at the mercy of the minority. Ten men can destroy a thousand if the thousand will only defend themselves one at a time.

In this tragedy the thousand, in the presence of the criminal violence of a small group have said: "Let each of us defend himself individually, not as a unit, a group, a corporate body against this criminal gang of ten." Thus, the ten in reality faced *one,* not a thousand at any given moment, for the remainder of the thousand were neutral. The thousand, which could have disposed of the ten quite easily, were destroyed.

The foregoing pages have tried to explain how it came about that men arrived at this strange conclusion that defense is best undertaken individually, a conclusion which on the face of it defies not only the elementary strategy of defense, but almost defies arithmetic itself. The book has tried to give some hint of the confusions which underlie it all and has ascribed the cause more to confusion, blunders, than the conscious motive of wickedness.

But there is, after all, something more than confusion, logical error, present in the tragedy. If there is such a thing as a "moral instinct," a conscience, a force which impels men to do the right thing, then that instinct must have become perverted or deadened. For the decision just indicated implies not only strategical miscalculation, it implies a repudiation of the truth that we are members one of another; that, as members of the same human family, threatened by the blind destructive forces not only of the external world, but by the even more destructive forces of human nature, its tempers, animosities, lusts, ferocities, retaliations, we must at some points stand together against evil, or go under.

You are walking with a friend down the street and encounter two hefty ruffians, who, to the entertainment of a surrounding crowd, are lustily pounding each other. You have no means of knowing what the rumpus is about, who began it, who is to blame; you are justified in walking on, and can usefully forget it. Neither you, nor your friend, nor your community will be morally any the worse for your "neutrality."

But the next day you come upon a couple of jack-booted brutes kicking an old woman in the gutter, smashing her face to pulp; a surrounding crowd finding that an entertainment too. Will you join that crowd of onlookers and decide that what happens to the old woman is no affair of yours? Even though the next day you encounter the same thing or something like it; and the next, and the next, and the next, and on one occasion a child being defiled? Do you join the onlookers and decide that really it is no affair of yours, and that as a member of an orderly and humane community you need not move to have that community do anything about it? If that is indeed the choice of the onlookers, of those who make up the community, do you really believe that that will be the end of the matter? That that community can continue morally unchanged, however numerous become the beatings of the old women and the defilements of the children? Is our moral sense quite sound when we decide that the only criminals in this case are the men with the jack boots and the rubber truncheons?

Many Englishmen were deeply concerned, deeply moved when Japan seized Manchuria, attacked China after a gross "frame up" of manufactured atrocities and grievances, and Britain did nothing about it. Those Englishmen—who were so little listened to—pointed out that we had, after all, given China certain assurances, assumed certain obligations in respect of aid to her if she should become the victim of aggression; and that we could check the aggressor by extending aid to the victim. But the country was preoccupied with other things, the gold standard, the depression, and the national government. And really, "China's hands were not clean" (the phrase used by a Cabinet Minister). And Japan had been "an old and loyal ally" (another Ministerial phrase) and really you could never tell the rights and wrongs of these disputes. (At the moment the London police were spending twenty thousand pounds trying to find out who murdered a common prostitute, and no taxpayer thought of inquiring whether so expensive an enforcement of the law was permissible in the case of a victim of such doubtful character.) And then too we did not really have the force to check Japan (though everyone in those days knew, before the arrival of Hitler and the formation of the Axis, that if Japan were to attempt seizure of Hong Kong we should discover immediately that we *had* power to intervene). And also our purpose should be to localize wars, not spread them all over the map. And what were the Manchurians to us?

And so the aggression got nearer. Abyssinians followed Manchurians. And we decided that the Abyssinians were not very interesting either, that they ate raw meat and that Mussolini after all had made the trains keep time in Italy. So the mustard gas was taken through the Suez Canal, paid its dues, flayed alive naked peasants of

Abyssinia while Britain supplied material for the Italian forces wherewith to do it.

Sanctions? Well, yes, if they did not annoy Mussolini too much, for that might lead to war, and as our purpose was peace, we must let Italy have the oil. Mr. Churchill explained the policy of the government. "They tell us," he said, "that sanctions mean war; that the government will do nothing which might provoke war; and that its policy is sanctions." And so, of course, sanctions did not work. And then after Abyssinia, Spain. By every law, old or new, the Spanish government had the right to secure arms wherewith to defend itself. But Germany and Italy had made it plain that they were promoting the revolution against the Spanish government and that if Britain stood by the law—well, it would be the worse for Britain. It might mean war. And so, again said the government, we must avoid war above all else. So "Nonintervention" was invented and the Nonintervention Committee met in London. Nonintervention meant that there would be withdrawn from the Spanish government the right to secure arms for its defense, but that Germany and Italy should be free to supply the rebels with all the arms, all the equipment, all the technicians, all the armies that were necessary for the defeat of the government. The purpose of the Nonintervention Committee soon became evident. On a Monday Count Grandi would give a most solemn assurance that Italy was not intervening in Spain. On Tuesday Mussolini would send a long telegram—published in all the newspapers—addressed to the Commander of the Italian legionaries in Spain, congratulating them upon their glorious feat of arms in defeating the Communist hordes of the Spanish government. If some indiscreet member of the House of Commons wanted to know how the two things could be reconciled, he was informed that this came within the purview of the Committee of Nonintervention which unfortunately had adjourned for six weeks and it would be quite improper to make any statement in the meantime. British ships were sunk in considerable numbers and British seamen drowned, as the result of bombs and mysterious submarine torepdoes. The whole world knew that the bombs were German and the torpedoes Italian, but mention of the fact would disturb "friendly relations" then existing between

Italy and Britain. The one thing necessary was
to keep the peace, keep war from Britain's
shores. And so, the Nonintervention Committee
having done its work, Mr. Chamberlain and Lord
Halifax went to Rome and were entertained at
banquets by the man who had ordered the sinking
of British ships on their lawful occasions in
peacetime and the killing of peaceful civilians,
also in time of "peace." And the Duce's guests
smiled, and smiled, and smiled and talked of good
will and peace, and the common tasks of civilization. And Britain continued to nonintervene. And
in China, and Africa, and Spain, in the concentration camps of Germany men and women continued to perish for the crime of standing for
what all the world until yesterday had said was
Right; and old women continued to be kicked to
death and men of great and noble minds respected the world over fled from the Thing that
had come upon mankind, or, failing to flee, were
caught and tortured to death, mainly for the
crime of belonging to the race that gave us Jesus
Christ, His Mother, His Twelve Apostles and
the Ten Commandments. For the booted men
with the truncheons had proclaimed that either

Mary and the Son of Mary were Aryan, or ac-
cursed and His people outlawed.

And as people saw the pictures of the Duce's
smiling guests and read their fulsome speeches,
they said: It may be nauseating, but it is better
than war. Above all, keep us out of these quarrels
and wars that don't concern us. Keep out, keep
out, keep out.

But some said:

> This is not peace and cannot give us peace.
> We are trying to save ourselves by the sac-
> rifice of others whom we have obligations
> to defend; by sacrificing the innocent weak
> to the guilty strong. To say to these strong
> and evil men: "We will do nothing to de-
> fend the weak from the wrongs you inflict
> upon them, if you will solemnly promise
> not to inflict those wrongs upon us," is not
> only morally contemptible, it is politically
> imbecile. For the supply of innocent victims
> is strictly limited and the appetite of the
> aggressors is unlimited; it grows by the very
> ease of the triumphs we facilitate, by the
> booty we allow them to seize.

ALONE *OR* ALLIED?

But these Englishmen—although they included some of the great names of English politics, history and learning, names like Churchill, Cecil, Lytton, Toynbee, Gilbert Murray, Eden, Temple . . . were vilified as Warmongers, Disturbers of the Peace, Fomenters of Quarrels. They were plotting to "get the country into war" and we must KEEP OUT.

But the protestors were not the only unhappy ones. The people as a whole, especially the very common people, knew that this policy was wrong. Many were shocked in deep instincts of Right. And when after Manchuria, after Abyssinia, after the blasted cities of China, after the infamies of Spain, came Munich—"Peace in our time," based upon the solemn promise of Hitler that after the Sudetenland there would be no more conquests, no more occupations of neighboring territory— people knew that the end was drawing near.

It would be true to say that the stand was made over Poland—the very worst place and circumstances at which a stand against aggression could be made—because the capacity of the British people for supine surrender, surrender not of themselves, but of others, to armed evil was ex-

209

hausted. They could stomach no more. They would stand, though they perish—as perish so many of them will, as so many of them have. They would die upon their feet; but they would crawl no more; bow no more, smirk and smile no more, to what they know to be evil, vile and monstrous.

And now they fight alone. With greater wisdom, with an earlier moral insight, they could have had half a world standing with them, standing so that the evil thing perhaps would not even have raised its head at all.

It is the simple truth to say that because—either from indifference or from impatience—they turned their eyes away from the blazing homes of China, their own homes, some of them noble and ancient piles, every stone eloquent of English lore, of history and tradition, are now rubble heaps. Because they closed their ears to the cries of the children in Abyssinia and in Spain, they now hear the cries of their own children as the torpedoed vessel sinks six hundred miles from land.

It is the day of their atonement, nobly borne. The people who now fight are not the people who entered the war. They have changed. Bit by bit the men of Munich have been quietly squeezed out; eliminated into retirement, kicked upstairs into the House of Lords; and, more important than the men, are the values that have been changed; slowly, all too slowly. The things that were all important then, before the war, do not matter now; the things that are important now did not matter then.

And the common people of England have changed others besides themselves. It is amazing to see how in this distant America, certain fundamental moral assumptions, made universally but a year or two since, are made no more. The hardboiled materialism of the highbrows and the intellectuals, the cheap cynicisms are, for the time being at least, hushed. Here, too, there grows up a truer scale of values. Out of it may come a quicker grasp than England showed of what the price of freedom really is.

Chapter X

AMERICA CAN MAKE THE PEACE

Whether the next peace will be as defective as the last will depend upon America, for she will be the strongest nation at the settlement. Who will inherit the British Empire and the overseas Empires of France and Holland? If America inherits part management of this domain and makes good use of that inheritance, the world will still be safe for freedom. But it is the last chance.

A correspondent writes to a New York evening paper[1] thus:

The following letter I sent to the Committee to Defend America by Aiding the Allies:

"I should unhesitatingly sign your appeal to defend America by Aiding the Allies, or better at present Great Britain, if I were clear in regard to her war aims. It is all very well to say that Hitlerism must go, but what will be done if the world gets rid of him, an aim devotedly

[1] *PM,* October 4, 1940.

to be wished. We have once been cheated when we joined in a war against Germany, allegedly to save democracy . . . it seems to me that before getting involved more deeply in help to the Allies, Congress and the British Parliament should make a castiron treaty in regard to war aims: Is there going to be a vindictive peace if Germany should succumb? Will the warring nations make provision that with the necessary disarmament following the peace there will not be a most horrid period of misery in the countries of both vanquished and victors?

"If I could have assurance in regard to these points I should gladly join in your efforts. Notwithstanding my doubts of the ruling class in Great Britain, which antagonised republican Germany but pampered Hitler, and who have proved by their actions that they are at heart friends of Hitlerian policies, I acknowledge that the democratic tradition in England and my hatred of almost all that Hitler stands for is so strong that I connive at what is being done here; but before we go a single step further I want to know what England stands for."

One wonders whether this correspondent has considered what is certain to be the situation at the end of the war if Britain wins as the result of greatly increased aid extended now by the United States.

AMERICA'S DILEMMA:

Everyone knows the present economic situation of Great Britain. A great deal more than half of her entire national income goes already to the prosecution of the war. By the end of the war she will face utter economic exhaustion, and is likely to be dependent upon the United States for the very food wherewith to keep her population alive.

The victors on the next occasion will consist of the United States, with Britain dependent upon her, the British Dominions and certain states just liberated from Nazi control, dependent in their turn upon Britain, Britain being herself in a position of dependence.

In these circumstances the European states would hardly be able to move, to live, to carry on daily life, save by grace of the United States. Yet American commentators sometimes write as though America, sitting at the peace table, will be completely helpless as to the character of the peace which is to follow the victory her co-operation had produced.

The correspondent whose letter is reproduced above is greatly concerned to know what Britain is going to stand for at the peace. But as Great Britain would almost certainly not be able to enforce anything of her own power without regard to the United States; and, as the preponderance of power—the overwhelming preponderance of power—as between Britain and the United States will rest with the latter country, would it not be more pertinent to ask what the United States is going to stand for?

This attitude about being "cheated before" implies, of course, a mistaken conception of the nature of peace making and involves certain curious illusions.

At the close of the last war, there was a general demand for a "permanent settlement," once and for all, one that would be so just that it would never again be disturbed. It is about equivalent to saying:

> Let Congress make good laws for the United States once and for all; laws that will be fair and just for everybody; then let Congress and the Government shut up shop so that we can all go home and be left in peace never more to be bothered by these politicians.

Life and society are not so simple as that. There

can be no such thing as a permanent settlement "once for all." For what is just today will not be just tomorrow; or someone will not consider it just, and try to upset it by impatient violence if the condition of the world is such that impatient violence looks like being easy, easier than patient processes of peaceful change.

What was wrong with the Treaty of Versailles was much less the treaty than the course of policy in the years which followed it. The problem was in fact much less that of finding means for peaceful change than means of preventing changes by violence and aggression which did not make the *status quo* any better, but made it worse.

No man at this stage can forecast, even in outline, the conditions which a victorious America and Britain should or could lay down. The first problem is to prevent Germany laying down *her* peace terms. The first stage may be

1. So to "contain" Germany that the expansion of her power outside of the continent of Europe is decisively and definitely arrested.

2. By that fact to give hope to once free nations now under her domination, so that they may continue resistance—not necessarily military resist-

ance, but political resistance; so that the people of France, for instance, should not in hopelessness abandon themselves to the Nazification of their country through a puppet government, but should persist in the agitation which already exists. If Britain and America stand together undefeated, as proof and sign and symbol of the possibility of the successful resistance of free peoples to tyranny, then the steady political resistance by the peoples of Norway, Sweden, Denmark, Holland, Belgium, France, Poland, Spain, Greece, Yugoslavia, Roumania, Bulgaria to the Nazi regime is bound in the long run to present ever-increasing difficulty for the conqueror. One recalls what has been done in the way of resistance by little peoples to great, in the story of the Irelands, the Polands, the Finlands.

3. Since the proof of the possibility of resistance to the Nazi order will, in the event of American-British victory, be given by democratic peoples—democracies encircling the globe—the irredentist movement of the European peoples is almost certain to take a liberal and democratic rather than a communist turn. The Hitler youth, forming the nucleus of the Nazi party, may be

imbued successfully with the Nazi fanaticism. It will not be so easy to imbue conquered non-German peoples, Scandinavian, Dutch, French with that enthusiasm. Indeed none will know better than these the defects of the Nazi system, its mean tyrannies and dark horrors. Nor are they likely to forget that the other form of totalitarianism, the Communist form, betrayed them to the Nazi conqueror. But for Moscow, Hitler could not have marched upon them.

Hitler is aware, if Britain and America are not, that to confine his system to the Continent, while the democratic system is still living and vigorous in the Western Hemisphere, in Britain and the antipodes; remains a living and vivid aspiration in India and China, is in the end to frustrate the Nazi "revolution" and make the new order unworkable.

So long as Britain and America between them can command the sea, and agree upon the common defense of their common heritage, the preponderance of potential power and resource is still heavily against Nazidom.

ALONE *OR* ALLIED?

Think what the British-American world means:

First, unquestioned preponderance upon the Western Hemisphere deriving from Canadian and United States territory in the North, the possession of all the best strategic points in the Caribbean, many in South America, including the command of the Cape Horn route; strong points in the Pacific, the Far East, the East Indies (with the reversion of the Dutch East Indies) ; included also in the system Australia, New Zealand, the whole of Africa (if Britain holds out in the Mediterranean), the potential alliance of the Chinese people, of the people of India.

Take one point, not commonly realized in the United States: The vastness of India's man power, natural resources and industrial plant and the contribution that these might make against the Nazi-Fascist forces. During the war of 1914-1918, India raised and equipped more than 1,000,000 men for service in the Middle East and other theaters of war. If this war goes on, as is quite possible, for another three or four years, India could put an even larger, thoroughly-equipped force into the field.

While agriculture remains the basis of the Indian economy, the country has rich resources of coal, iron, petroleum and manganese, to mention only the more important items of her mineral wealth. She also produces oil seeds, cotton, jute and silk, far in excess of normal domestic requirements.

Of direct concern to the production of war supplies, India has an important iron and steel industry, second only to that of Great Britain among the countries of the British Commonwealth. In 1939, for instance, India produced a monthly average of over 150,000 metric tons of pig iron and 85,000 tons of steel; her steel industry is now in the process of expansion designed to enable India to produce a million tons a year and, with the exception of a few special categories, meet the whole of her demands. The advance in the production of textiles has been particularly important; for example, India is now in a position to supply monthly almost as many sandbags as she did annually during the war of 1914-18. In 1931, more than 16,000,000 persons were engaged in industrial employment of one kind or another; at the present time the figure is far greater.

ALONE *OR* ALLIED?

In modern warfare, between 35,000 and 40,000 items are required by a mechanized army. More than half these are now being produced in India; small arms, ammunition, shells, rifles and machine guns, field and A.A. guns, bombs and mines are being manufactured on an important scale, and the various works engaged in producing them are being rapidly expanded. In 1936, India was making more than 90 per cent of the requirements of her armed forces, the chief exceptions being motor transports and airplanes. It would not be at all surprising if India were producing large numbers of aircraft before the war is over. Steps have already been taken toward this goal and, while there are great difficulties to be overcome and time is needed to set up machines and organize plants, the Chinese government has shown, during the last three years, what can be done in this direction.

If the Near East becomes a major theater of war, the part which India can play in this great life and death struggle becomes more important than ever before. India's fighting men, her guns and munitions, may one day prove a deciding factor in the struggle in the Mediterranean area where it should be possible to deal a staggering blow to the enemy. Incidentally, the more difficult it becomes for Britain to keep open the lines of communication through the Mediterranean, the more vital will it be for Britain to be able to secure reinforcements and supplies from India.

A start has already been made on building up an Indian air force and there are plenty of eager young volunteers anxious to earn their "wings." An authority who knows the Indians extremely well has high hopes for this branch of the fighting forces. As airmen who might be called upon to deal with the Fascist air force in the Near East, he believes that Indians would be more than a match for the best Italian pilots; as individuals, the Indians are capable of outstanding acts of bravery and indifference to danger and death.

Regardless of differences on constitutional questions, Indians are united in their loathing of all that Nazism and Fascism stand for. Constitutional issues, important as they are, are secondary. If the Nazi-Fascist challenge were not met successfully, constitutional issues wouldn't matter very much either at Westminster or Delhi.[2]

[2] I owe this sketch of the Indian situation to Commander King-Hall.

I have gone at some length into the Indian possibilities because it raises the question of how far the British Commonwealth and the American Union are to be associated in the future in their common defense. We are already greatly "mixed up" as Churchill put it. And in the deal about the naval bases Britain has taken a step unlike that ever perhaps taken by one nation toward another in the past. "Defense" has commonly meant building barriers against the entrance of neighbors to your territory. Britain has done, in respect of the United States, the exact reverse. She has said to the United States:

> "Come in and add to your strength on our territory; make yourself strong within our lines."

Every week seems to add some new feature of common action for mutual defense.

That common action must, of course, continue long after the Nazi thrust against the West has been repelled. It may take some permanent form along the lines which Mr. Clarence Streit has so ably, successfully and usefully advocated. But men are sometimes more afraid of names than of things. "Alliance" sounds terrifying to many; "Union" less so to some, more so to others. But whether we call it Union or Alliance, or Federation, or Confederation, or Association is really of less importance than common realization of the principles upon which we should act in the framing of the post-Hitler peace.

The basic principle of that peace should be as regards Germany this. We should say in effect:

> We do not ask you to accept our dictation or domination, any more than we should be prepared to accept yours. We ask you to accept the domination of a law or principle of international life by which we ourselves are prepared to abide. That law is that no nation, in its disputes with others, shall impose its partial and interested judgment by war, or threat of war and by using war to wipe out the national life of its neighbors. That we shall oppose by all the aid to the victim of violence that we can give.

That is not the whole problem of peace, but it is its foundation. That foundation the United States and the British Commonwealth must lay together, whatever name they may give to their association, whatever precise form it may take.

Of course, the peace may be muddled; and, of course, difficulties will arise which will make the peace defective. It may possibly be very defective, even if we do stop Hitler. But then if we don't stop Hitler, we know for a dead certainty that the peace will be quite intolerable. And when in life you have to choose between one course, which may not result in all the success that you hope, but will at least be tolerable and another course which you know to a dead certainty will be disastrous and completely intolerable, then you choose the former course.

In life and politics, it is never a choice, as has been insisted upon more than once in these pages, between something entirely good and something entirely bad; something entirely white and something unrelievably black. But when you have made your choice, because, when all is said and done, one choice is plainly much better than the other, then you have to back that decision with the same relentless vigor as though the cause for which you fight were spotless.

If you don't do that; if you decide that you will

only be a little energetic on behalf of the right course, while an opponent is going all out on behalf of the wrong, then you will be beaten. And one of the outstanding lessons of the dreadful tragedy of our time is that somehow evil seems to have rallied to itself more sacrifice, devotion and singleness of purpose than good has managed to rally. It would seem that energy is for evil only.

The lesson which Europe failed to learn is the lesson of the necessary co-operations. Each nation refused that co-operation on the ground that its first duty was to its own people. By that error, which it called "realism," each destroyed its own people. Will the same "realism" destroy the United States? America has now the chance to learn from the errors of others, to avoid the pits into which they have fallen. But it is almost certainly the last chance so to learn.